FISH & SEAFOOD MASTERPIECES

Cooking Arts Collection™

CREDITS

About the Author

Chef John Schumacher has an extraordinary range of culinary experience, specializing in wild game, fish and Central European cuisine. Internationally known, John has authored several cookbooks, including *Wild Game Cooking Made Easy*, *John Schumacher's New Prague Hotel Cookbook* and *Today's Country Cooking*. He lives in Minnesota, a place with many fish to catch, cook and eat.

FISH & SEAFOOD MASTERPIECES

Copyright ©2001 Cooking Club of America

Tom Carpenter, Director of Book Development

Dan Kennedy, Book Production Manager

Jen Guinea, Book Development Coordinator

Tad Ware & Company, Inc.,   Book Design and Production
Photography
Food Styling
Recipe Testing

Glenn Sapir, *Fish & Seafood Essentials* Research and Text

1 2 3 4 5 6 7 8 / 05 04 03 02 01
ISBN 158159-148-9

Cooking Club of America
12301 Whitewater Drive, Suite 260
Minnetonka, MN 55403
www.cookingclub.com

TABLE OF CONTENTS

$\mathcal{I}$NTRODUCTION

Mystique surrounds fish and seafood cooking.

Some of the mystery is appropriate: Here are these finned and shelled creatures of the deep, from both fresh and salt water, that are delicately flavored and, yes, a little demanding on the stove or grill, or in the oven or pot.

But therein lies some of the attraction. And, cooked right, fish and seafood can become some of the most delightful and rewarding dishes you've ever created. The challenge is approachable, even conquerable. That's what *Fish & Seafood Masterpieces* is all about.

To start, we'll discuss some of the secrets of buying and storing fish and seafood for maximum freshness — one of the simple keys to great taste. Then we'll cover the basics of each cooking technique, as it pertains to fish and seafood. Once we've covered these ground rules, it's time to jump into the recipes.

Many recipes purposely don't identify which fish to use, because I don't want to keep you from trying other fish, or limiting yourself in any way. What's more important is the size and thickness of the piece of fish — that

it makes sense with the cooking technique and time outlined.

And remember. Fish is worth fussing over. This doesn't mean a recipe has to be difficult; most of these ideas aren't! But it does mean that fish is delicate, and not very forgiving. Use only fresh fish as much as possible … and don't overcook. You can always take it back to the heat — but you can't uncook it!

As for cooking shellfish, freshness is the watchword too. In this age of jet travel and just-in-time supply lines to markets, you shouldn't have any problem getting incredibly fresh seafood, no matter where you live. Shop where everybody else does so you know the inventory is turning over often.

When cooking shellfish, the fish-cooking rule also applies: Don't overdo it or you'll dry the meat into a bland and tasteless disappointment. And avoid heavy, spicy, exotic or overwhelming sauces over shellfish; you'll taste only that and not what's supposed to be the dish's real star.

No, this isn't your traditional fish and seafood cookbook. The chapters are mostly centered on traditional fish and seafood preparation techniques — baking, roasting, pan-frying, sautéing — but the recipes are far from ordinary. You'll also find soups and chowders (and not just a token recipe or two), grilling, salads, sandwiches … all kinds of ideas you might never have expected in a fish and seafood cookbook. Spread your wings and try it all!

If you make these recipes and feel good, then I will feel good. Enjoy *Fish & Seafood Masterpieces*!

— Chef John

GOLDEN TROUT

YELLOW TAIL

FISH & SEAFOOD ESSENTIALS

Great fish and seafood meals start with fresh ingredients; keeping them fresh and wholesome, until you're ready to cook, is also key. It helps to know proper and proven cleaning techniques as well... and understand the basics of each cooking method.

Excellent fish and seafood meals start with fresh, wholesome ingredients… chief of which are, of course, the feature finned or shelled creatures you are buying. These tips and suggestions will help you get off to a delicious and healthful beginning.

BUYING FRESH FISH

Selecting fresh fish is important for taste and health reasons. Never be afraid to ask the store or shop's proprietor when he received the fish. Your own educated senses can also be a reliable barometer of freshness.

In examining a whole fish, look at its eyes. They should be clear and shiny, with a slight bulge. The pupil should be black, the cornea translucent. Beware of eyes that appear cloudy and sunken. The gills should seem moist and appear red or bright pink. The skin should be shiny, and its color should not have faded.

If you are considering a fillet, it should look moist, and evenly firm with an elastic texture. On both fillets and steaks, bloodlines should be red. Gaps in the flesh shouldn't exist. Dark spots, bruises or yellowing around the edges should discourage purchase.

Using your sense of smell, sniff for a fresh and mild scent. The fish should not smell "fishy."

Fish should never be slimy to the touch. The flesh should bounce back if you touch it, attesting to its firmness.

BUYING FROZEN FISH

Believe it or not, senses can play an equally important role in selecting quality frozen fish. Look for solidly frozen flesh. Make sure that there is no discoloration, brownish tinge or white cotton-like appearance (indicating freezer burn). The wrapper should be perfectly intact, offering a total moisture/vapor shield, with little or no air space between the fish and the wrapping. Note, however, that a glaze of ice may protect some whole fish, shrimp and salmon and halibut steaks.

Smell the package too. Odor should be nonexistent or slight.

BUYING FRESH SHELLFISH

Smell is important in evaluating the freshness of shellfish. For example, shrimp should have an ocean scent. When shrimp spoil, the smell is trapped in the shell. Brown shrimp, especially large ones, suggest a high content of iodine. It is naturally occurring, but may offend sensitive palates. Avoid shrimp with black spots on their shell. Likewise, yellow shells or gritty-feeling shells may suggest the prior use of sodium bisulfite to remove those black spots.

Clams, oysters, mussels and scallops in the shell must be alive. If you tap the shells, they should close tightly. Open shells suggest the shellfish is dead and inedible.

Shucked oysters should have only a mild odor. The flesh is usually creamy in color, accompanied by a clear "nectar."

Scallops in packages should have a sweetish odor with no excess liquid.

Telltale signs of less-than-healthy lobsters are droopy claws and tail, and they may show little or no reaction when handled.

BUYING SHRIMP

Though shrimp come by different names to describe their size, the best way to understand size is to determine how many you get to a pound. Here's a handy chart describing different size shrimp and their uses.

Count per Pound	Common Name	Use
12	Colossal	Stuffing and grilling
16 to 20	Jumbo	Appetizers, poaching, stuffing and grilling
21 to 25	Large	Appetizers, poaching, soups, pastas and sautés
26 to 30	Medium	Soups, pastas and sautés
41 to 50	Small	Same as "Medium"
70 or more	Salad or Extra Small	Mayonnaise-based salads or pureed for stuffing

STORING FISH AND SHELLFISH

Unfortunately, you can't always prepare a meal as soon as you get home from a fishing excursion or the market. Properly storing fish is an essential, preliminary step in cooking a delicious finfish or shellfish meal. Follow these guidelines and everything should be as fresh as can be, and taste great.

STORING FRESH-CAUGHT FISH

Lots of people go fishing these days, either on their own or maybe with a guide or charter boat. What a great opportunity for superb fish meals! Here's what to do.

1. Clean freshly caught fish and place them in a cooler of ice as soon as possible after the catch.
2. At home, wash fish to remove scales or foreign matter.
3. Line the storage container bottom with a layer of ice. Cover the ice with plastic, and then lay the whole fish or fillets on the plastic. Place another sheet of plastic, then another layer of ice over the fish. Store on the bottom shelf of the refrigerator, and replace ice as it melts. Be sure to prevent contact between the fish and the ice.
4. The fish can be stored like this from four to six days, though two days is preferred. After a day, however, you should wash fillets before cooking them.

STORING FRESH-PURCHASED FISH

Dockside fish and seafood markets are great places to purchase fresh fish. Try your local markets — they may offer a fresh catch or two. Once home, follow these guidelines for storing your purchase.

1. Wash fish to remove scales and foreign matter.
2. Place fish you've purchased in a 35°F to 40°F refrigerator in original leak-proof wrapping as soon as possible after purchase.
3. Store no longer than two days before cooking.
4. If you plan on eating the fish more than two days after purchasing, go ahead and freeze it immediately after you get it home.

HOW MUCH FISH TO BUY

Here are some guidelines on how much fish or seafood, or how many shellfish, you should be buying. Notice that as the fish becomes more processed, you need to purchase less "poundage."

Fish or Seafood	Amount
Whole Fish	¾ to 1 lb. per person
Dressed or Clean Fish	½ to ¾ lb. per person
Fillets and Steaks	⅓ to ½ lb. per person
Live Lobster and Crabs	1 to 2 lb. per person
Mussels	12 to 15 per person
Oysters and Clams	6 to 12 per person, depending on size (of the oysters or clams, and the diners' appetites!)

FREEZING FISH

Whether you've caught and cleaned them or bought them at the store or market, follow these rules when freezing fish:

1. Clean and rinse the fish, then pat dry with a paper towel.
2. Freeze small fish in one piece. Cut larger fish into 1-inch-thick steaks or small fillets.
3. Wrap tightly in plastic wrap, squeezing out any trapped air.
4. Wrap again in aluminum foil.
5. Write the contents and date on a freezer label or masking tape strip.
6. Freeze as quickly as possible (0°F is optimum freezer temperature).

FISH FREEZING TIP

Frozen the traditional way, fish can be in the freezer for a few months without getting freezer burn. To lengthen freezer time and retain optimum taste, you may decide to freeze fish inside a water-filled milk container or zipper-sealed plastic bag. Simply place the fish in the container and fill with water to one inch of the top. That allows room for expansion. The ice does not allow air to penetrate to the fish. With this method, fish will retain its flavor for at least one year, maybe even two.

STORING FROZEN FISH

Place commercially packaged frozen fish, in their original wrapper, in the freezer immediately after purchase.

Store in a freezer at 0°F or lower. In temperatures above that, fish can lose color, flavor, texture and nutrients.

Store for no longer than two months.

STORING FRESH & FROZEN SHELLFISH

Shellfish die if they are stored at a temperature much higher or lower than 32°F. In addition, if they are covered with fresh water for an extended period of time, they will die.

- Store fresh shellfish at approximately 32°F. It is best to eat fresh shellfish on the day of purchase.
- Keep live mussels, scallops, clams and oysters in a container with drainage holes, cover with a towel, then cover with ice. Do not allow ice to make contact with the shellfish.
- Keep in a cool, damp place, but not the refrigerator.

STORING COOKED FISH & SHELLFISH

Once you've cooked them, fish and shellfish can be saved for another meal.

- Store in the refrigerator in a covered container for no more than two or three days.
- Store in the freezer in a moisture/vapor-proof package for no longer than three months.

THAWING FROZEN FISH

Do not thaw fish at room temperature. Instead thaw it in the refrigerator. Here's how:

1. If you've frozen the fish in ice, remove the block of ice encasing the fish from its container.
2. Run cold water over the ice to melt it.
3. When the ice has melted, place the fish on a paper towel and put it in a container.
4. Cover the container with plastic wrap and complete the thawing process in the refrigerator.

$\mathcal{C}$LEANING AND PREPARING FISH

A fish is at its top table quality as soon as it is caught. Taste deteriorates from that moment on, but you can maximize taste and minimize deterioration by handling fresh-caught fish correctly from the moment it comes out of the water. These fish-cleaning rules also apply to fish you purchase. You can also fillet your fish, and we'll show you how to do that. And we'll show you how to properly prepare shellfish.

CLEANING FISH

Whether you catch them or buy them, here's how to treat fish so that they taste great.

1. Handle fish gently, preventing bruising. Dispatch them immediately. Cut them at the gills to bleed them. Keep them out of the sun, and put them on ice as soon as possible.
2. Clean, dress and steak or fillet them as soon as possible.
3. Scale or skin fish as required. Remove scales by scraping with a specialized tool, dull knife or spoon, going from the tail toward the head.
4. If you decide to skin the fish, scaling is not necessary. To skin, split the skin at the top of the back and loosen it around the fins. With pliers, remove the skin, pulling from head to tail.

5. To dress a fish, make a cut along the belly, from the vent hole to the head. Remove viscera and gills, if you are keeping the head on (as with trout). If you wish to remove the head, cut it off above the gills. Remove the dorsal fin by cutting along each side and pulling out the fin and attached bones. If you simply trim the fins, bones at the base of the fins will remain.

6. Wash the fish thoroughly in cold running water. Use only drinking-quality water.

STEAKING FISH

Steaking a fish is easy. Steaking won't remove bones, like filleting does, but that often doesn't matter in the large fish — like salmon — that are steaked. To steak the fish, simply cut the fish crosswise into 1-inch-thick portions.

FILLETING A FISH

To fillet fish, you may skip all the steps previously mentioned, because in this process you will remove the internal viscera as well as the skin.

1. Cut behind the pectoral fin and gill cover down to the backbone. Angle the cut toward the top of the head so you don't waste the thick meat behind the head.

2. Make a cut along one side of the back; the tip of your knife blade should just scrape the rib bones but not cut through them.

3. When your knife reaches the end of the rib cage, push the knife all the way through the fish and then run it along the backbone to free the rear portion of the fillet.

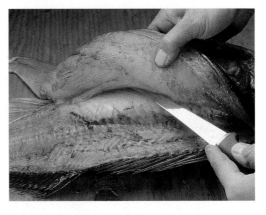

4. Make a series of light cuts around the outside of the rib cage to remove the rest of the fillet. Keep the blade as close to the ribs as possible so you don't waste meat. Turn the fish over and repeat the procedure to remove the other fillet.

5. To skin a fillet, lay it skin side-down on a cutting board. Hold the tail end with your fingers and cut through the flesh near the tail. Run the knife forward while holding the free end of the skin firmly between your fingers.

PREPARING SHRIMP

If you are going to prepare shrimp in a hot liquid, you should remove the shell first. Pry open and pull back the first few sections of shell, starting at the large end. Remove the rest of the shell by gently tugging on the end of the shrimp's tail.

If you are grilling or boiling the shrimp, don't remove the shell. The shell protects the meat and imparts a desirable flavor.

Deveining shrimp is not really necessary, but some people prefer to do it. The "sand vein" is actually the shrimp's digestive tract. It is harmless to eat, but may have a slightly gritty texture.

Here's how to devein the shrimp:

1. Without peeling the shell, simply cut down the back of the shrimp with kitchen shears.

2. Remove the vein with the tip of a paring knife. You may prefer to use a tool especially made for deveining. It is available in a kitchen-supply store.

BUTTERFLYING SHRIMP

If you would like to evenly cook shrimp by flattening them, or you would like to stuff the shrimp, you should "butterfly" them. Slice just deep enough to open each shrimp without cutting it in half.

These cooking strategies, guidelines and techniques will prove themselves valuable when you create the recipes that follow, and when you decide to go "solo" and try some fish and seafood creations of your own.

PAN FRYING AND SAUTEING

Pan frying or sautéing is recommended for fish fillets less than 1¼ inches thick, shucked oysters, large shrimp and scallops. These two cooking methods are very similar. Use a skillet with a nonstick surface to reduce need for excessive oil or lard. Pat fish dry to minimize splattering during cooking. If desired, dust in chosen coating. Cook over medium high heat. Brown seafood on one side, then turn over to cook the other side. A general rule is to cook 10 minutes per inch of thickness. Consider cooking for about six minutes on the first side, four minutes on the second.

When sautéing:

1. Use a very light coating of flour on the fish.
2. Heat one tablespoon of butter and one tablespoon of cooking oil in a skillet over medium high heat.

When pan frying:

1. Coat fish with flour, cornmeal, breadcrumbs or finely chopped nuts that will create a crispy coating, while leaving the inside meat moist and tender.
2. Use cooking oil, not butter, to a depth of ⅛ to ¼ inch. Add fish and cook until browned. Turn the fish and cook until browned on the outside, opaque at the thickest part.

MICROWAVING

Microwaving is recommended for someone looking to prepare a quick, easy meal.

- Microwave the fish for 5 to 10 minutes on High power. Cooking time varies with how much fish you're cooking, and how big the pieces are.
- Allow more time for thick fillets and whole fish. If the fish still has its skin, place it skin side down. Slash the skin to prevent curling. Place thicker pieces along the outer edge of baking dish so the fish will cook evenly.

• Cover the cooking dish tightly with plastic wrap. Allow the fish to stand for five minutes, while venting one corner to allow steam to escape.

GRILLING

Grilling is recommended for a variety of steaks and fillets, and is especially good for cod, salmon, shrimp, lobster, scallops and mussels. Be careful when grilling — don't overdo it and dry out the fish or shellfish. Remember you can always put it back on, but you can't uncook it.

• Oil the grate before adding the fish. This helps prevent the fish from sticking to the grill.

• Marinate fish steaks or lightly brush them with oil. Place steaks directly on the grill and cook for 5 to 7 minutes, or until ready. Readiness can be determined by noting when the fish turns from translucent to opaque in the center.

• To prevent fillets from flaking apart, carefully cook them on a grilling rack or on foil. Fillets with skin may be placed directly on the grill, skin-side down. Cook until done, basting as needed. Grill for 10 minutes per inch of thickness.

• Thread shrimp and scallops, alternating with vegetables on skewers. Grill for two to three minutes on each side.

POACHING

Poaching is recommended for scallops, shrimp, shucked oysters, whole fish, fish fillets and steaks. Poaching is the simple technique of placing fish in a hot liquid. The result is flavorful fish with no added fat. You may use water with seasonings and herbs, fish stock or wine.

1. Use a broad, shallow pan that can accommodate the fish in an even layer, but do not place the fish in the pan.

2. Place enough seasoned liquid to completely cover the fish. Bring liquid to a rolling boil, and then reduce the heat so that no bubbles break the surface.

3. Add the fish, but do not cover the pan. Poach until the fish is cooked in the center.

STEAMING

Steaming is recommended for the same fish as for the poaching technique. Steaming also avoids the addition of extra fat from butter or cooking oil.

- Use a steamer or substitute with a cake rack in a roasting pan.
- The difference between poaching and steaming is that when steaming, you keep the fish above the liquid, not in it. Steam about 10 minutes per inch of thickness.

STIR-FRYING

Stir-frying is recommended for strips or cubes of firm fish such as halibut, monkfish, salmon, swordfish, tuna and shark, as well as shrimp, scallops and squid.

This method cooks small pieces over high heat. Because the food cooks quickly, it requires constant stirring to even out how everything cooks and to avoid sticking to the pan. Do not use delicate fish, because it will fall apart. Do not overcrowd the pan, or the fish will release liquid and poach, rather than fry. Cooking batches of fish avoids the problem. A wok or skillet is ideal.

Here's how to stir fry:

1. Warm the oil in a wok or large skillet over high heat. If using vegetables, add them first and cook them very quickly, stirring constantly. When vegetables are tender-crisp, transfer them to a bowl and set them aside.
2. Add more oil to the pan if necessary and reheat. Add the fish and cook, stirring until done — browned on the outside, opaque in the center.
3. Return the vegetables to the pan, add any sauce or seasoning and stir them to evenly mix and re-warm the combination of vegetables and fish.

Sometimes you'll discover it is more convenient to find a recipe than the fish that the recipe calls for! All is not lost, however, because different varieties of both finfish and shellfish can often be substituted. The recipes to come keep this in mind: Use the fish you can get! To aid you in determining what might work best, follow these guidelines:

- Perhaps the most economical substitution is for **lobster**. **Monkfish** is a finfish often referred to as "poor man's lobster." It can be used in any recipe calling for lobster. Monkfish can also substitute for **scallops**.

- **Triggerfish**, found off the Carolina coast, is an excellent substitute for grouper. It is mild and flaky like grouper, but has an even sweeter taste — and it costs less too.

- **Mako shark** might not have quite the flavor of **swordfish**, but it can serve as a fair substitute in recipes.

- **Flatfish** are often interchangeable. **Winter flounder** can replace **summer flounder**, the latter also called **fluke**. **Gray sole** can also serve as a substitute.

- Recipes calling for **haddock** can work for **cod** as well.

- **Salmon** can substitute for the hard-to-get **Arctic char**.

- **Red snapper** can be substituted with a Venezuelan fish sold at American markets. It is known as a **beeliner** or **South American red snapper**.

- **Bluefish** has a dark, oily flesh. **American shad** can serve as an alternative.

- **Largemouth** and **smallmouth bass** are interchangeable.

- **Northern pike** and **pickerel** are in the pike family. They may be substituted for one another. Watch out for the "Y" bones!

- **Panfish** such as **bluegills, pumpkinseeds** and other **sunfish** may be substituted for one another, as can **crappies**.

- **Rainbow trout** are the most common commercially sold trout species, but **brown**, **brook** and **cutthroat trout** are interchangeable in recipes calling for trout. **Lake trout**, however, are generally larger and their fillets thicker than the other species.

- **Catfish** are firm, white-fleshed fish. Most any other white-fleshed fish makes an acceptable substitute. **Channel catfish** are most common, many being raised on fish farms or netted commercially.

- **Walleye** is a savored freshwater food fish, but when it is not available, **yellow perch** — a smaller family member of the walleye family — is a superb substitute in taste (some say it's better!), if not in size.

STARTERS

Don't ignore fish when planning appetizers and starters for any occasion. Breakfast and brunch are starters in their own right too… you'll find a few of those types of recipes inside this chapter as well.

Oysters on the Half Shell with Honza Sauce, page 35

BREAKFAST FISH SOUFFLE

If you are a risk taker, this is your kind of cooking. But soufflés are always well worth the risk.

1½ cups half-and-half
½ cup each diced onions, celery, bell pepper (¼ inch thick)
1½ teaspoons fresh thyme
1 garlic clove, quartered
6 black peppercorns
1 cup diced boneless skinless fish fillets (½ inch thick)
¼ cup butter
2 tablespoons all-purpose flour

1 tablespoon German mustard
Dash each salt, ground white pepper
2 cups (8 oz.) shredded sharp cheddar cheese
5 egg yolks
7 egg whites, room temperature
1 tablespoon freshly grated Parmesan cheese

❶ Heat oven to 350°F. Butter and flour 2½-quart soufflé dish. In medium saucepan, simmer half-and-half, onions, celery, bell pepper, thyme, garlic and peppercorns over medium heat 3 minutes. Do not boil. Remove from heat; let stand 15 minutes to infuse flavors.

❷ Strain onion mixture, reserving liquid in small saucepan. Add cubed fish; simmer 3 minutes. With slotted spoon, place fish in medium bowl to cool. Reserve liquid.

❸ In large skillet, heat butter to a fast bubble over medium-high heat. Stir in flour; cook 1 minute, stirring constantly. Remove from heat. Stir in reserved liquid, whipping until smooth with wire whisk. Return mixture to heat; cook until a smooth, thick sauce forms. Stir in mustard, salt, pepper and cheese. Remove from heat. Cool 5 minutes. With wooden spoon, stir in egg yolks, one at a time, until well blended.

❹ In clean large bowl, beat egg whites until stiff. With wire whisk, slowly fold cheese mixture into egg whites. Gently combine, being careful not to over mix.

❺ Pour one-half of egg mixture into soufflé dish. Very gently place fish evenly in mixture. Top with remaining egg mixture. Bake 30 minutes. Sprinkle Parmesan over crust. Bake an additional 10 minutes or until set. Serve soufflé immediately.

4 servings.

Preparation time: 1 hour. Ready to serve: 1 hour, 45 minutes.

Per serving: 620 calories, 48 g total fat (28 g saturated fat), 415 mg cholesterol, 765 mg sodium, 0 g fiber.

SAUTEED FISH WITH ALMOND PESTO

Pesto is an uncooked sauce originally from Genoa, Italy. It is made with herbs, nuts, grated hard cheese and olive oil, and creates a truly unique flavor.

1/4   cup *Clarified Butter* (page 167)
1   cup *Seasoned Flour* (page 170)
4   cups diced boneless skinless fish fillets
2   teaspoons fresh lemon juice
1   cup *Almond Pesto* (see recipe)

> **CHEF'S NOTE:**
> • Fish fillets must be handled gently to retain their shape. If you are not concerned with the shape, use whole panfish fillets.

❶ In large skillet, heat Clarified Butter to a fast bubble over medium-high heat.

❷ Place Seasoned Flour in 9-inch pie plate. Gently coat fillets with Seasoned Flour, shaking off excess. Place fillets in skillet; sauté until golden brown and fillets flake easily with a fork. Sprinkle evenly with lemon juice.

❸ Heat large dinner plate. Spread plate with warm Almond Pesto. Top with fillets.

4 servings.

Preparation time: 5 minutes. Ready to serve: 15 minutes.

Per serving: 795 calories, 63 g total fat (16 g saturated fat), 130 mg cholesterol, 860 mg sodium, 3 g fiber.

ALMOND PESTO

1/2   cup unsalted whole almonds
2   teaspoons plus 2/3 cup extra-virgin olive oil
2   garlic cloves, finely minced
1/8   teaspoon salt
1/4   teaspoon grated lime peel
1/8   teaspoon freshly ground 3-pepper blend
2   cups chopped fresh basil
1/4   cup (1 oz.) freshly grated Parmesan cheese

> **CHEF'S NOTE:**
> • If you are a purist, use pine nuts instead of almond slices.

❶ To roast almonds, roll almonds in 2 teaspoons of the oil. Place on baking sheet. Bake at 350°F 10 minutes. Cool.

❷ In blender, puree remaining 2/3 cup oil, roasted almonds, garlic, salt, lime peel and pepper blend on low speed 30 seconds. Add basil; puree until basil is finely chopped. Add Parmesan cheese; puree to combine.

❸ Place puree in container; cover and store in refrigerator.

1 cup.

SHRIMP NACHOS

This recipe should not be legal! Once you prepare and eat shrimp nachos, you will do anything to keep eating them.

- 2 cups diced tomatoes (1/4 inch thick)
- 1 cup diced dill pickles (1/4 inch thick)
- 6 cups extra-large corn chips
- 8 shelled deveined jumbo shrimp, quartered
- 1/3 cup sliced ripe olives
- 1/2 cup guacamole
- 1/2 cup sour cream
- 1 cup (4 oz.) shredded sharp cheddar cheese
- 1/2 cup salsa
- 1/2 cup diced green onions (1/4 inch thick)
- 2 to 3 chiles of choice, sliced (1/8 inch thick)

> **CHEF'S NOTE:**
> • Add 2 cups of shredded lettuce to this recipe before adding the cheddar cheese.

❶ Heat oven to 375°F.

❷ Place tomatoes and pickles in strainer; drain off excess liquid.

❸ Place corn chips in ovenproof serving dish. Top with shrimp, tomatoes, pickles, olives, guacamole, sour cream, cheddar cheese, salsa, onions and chiles. Bake 15 minutes or until shrimp turn pink.

4 servings.

Preparation time: 20 minutes. Ready to serve: 35 minutes.

Per serving: 515 calories, 35 g total fat (12.5 g saturated fat), 90 mg cholesterol, 1255 mg sodium, 7 g fiber.

MUSHROOMS AND SCALLOPS KATHLEEN

This is the most popular appetizer at our restaurant. Kathleen is my wife.

12	large mushroom caps
1¼	lb. butter, softened
¼	cup thick-sliced cooked bacon, crumbled
¼	cup minced shallots
1	tablespoon chopped fresh parsley
6	garlic cloves, minced
12	large sea scallops

❶ Heat oven to 350°F.

❷ Place mushroom caps, hollow side up, in 3-quart casserole. In medium bowl, combine butter, bacon, shallots, parsley and garlic; mix well. Place 1 teaspoon garlic-butter mixture in each mushroom cap; top with 1 scallop. Cover each mushroom with 1 rounded tablespoon garlic-butter mixture.

❸ Bake 20 minutes or until golden brown and scallops turn opaque. Serve with toast points.

4 servings.

Preparation time: 20 minutes. Ready to serve: 40 minutes.

Per serving: 600 calories, 60 g total fat (36.5 g saturated fat), 170 mg cholesterol, 540 mg sodium, 1g fiber.

CHEF'S NOTES:

• Pine nuts can be substituted for bacon.

• If you're adventurous, add 1 shrimp per mushroom cap. For a more complex taste, add 1 escargot per mushroom cap.

• For fish-stuffed mushrooms, use 1-inch boneless skinless fish pieces.

LACY CHEESE FISH ROLL-UPS

This recipe marries Italian cheese with Mexican salsa to make a delicious fish!

¼ cup plus 1 tablespoon *Clarified Butter* (page 167)
½ cup *Seasoned Flour* (page 170)
4 boneless skinless fish fillets
2 tablespoons olive oil
½ cup diced red onions (¼ inch thick)
½ cup chopped ripe olives
4 artichoke hearts, halved
1½ cups salsa
2 cups (8 oz.) finely shredded Monterey Jack cheese
1 cup (4 oz.) finely shredded Swiss cheese

❶ In large skillet, heat ¼ cup of the Clarified Butter to a fast bubble over medium-high heat. Place Seasoned Flour in 9-inch pie plate. Dredge fillets in Seasoned Flour, shaking off excess. Place fillets in skillet; fry until golden brown and flaky. Place fillets on paper towel-lined plate. Cover to keep warm.

❷ In another large skillet, heat oil over medium-high heat until hot. Add onions, olives and artichoke hearts; sauté until onions are transparent and tender. Add salsa; bring to a boil.

❸ Lightly brush bottom of medium skillet with remaining 1 tablespoon Clarified Butter. In medium bowl, combine Monterey Jack and Swiss cheeses; mix well. Place ¾ cup of the cheese mixture in skillet; melt over medium heat in thin circle. When cheese turns golden brown on bottom, top with fish fillet and ¼ cup salsa mixture. Fold in half; place on warm serving plate. Serve with remaining warm salsa mixture.

4 servings.
Preparation time: 10 minutes. Ready to serve: 25 minutes.
Per serving: 795 calories, 50 g total fat (25 g saturated fat), 235 mg cholesterol, 1430 mg sodium, 5 g fiber.

$\mathcal{I}$TALIAN-FISH STUFFED SHELLS

Served hot or cold, as an entrée or appetizer, these shells are worth the effort.

12 boneless skinless panfish fillets
 2 teaspoons lemon-pepper seasoning
12 (1x^1/2-inch) mozzarella cheese sticks
12 jumbo pasta shells
 1 tablespoon olive oil
 2 cups fresh mushrooms, halved
 1 cup diced red bell pepper (^{1}/2 inch thick)
 2 garlic cloves, finely minced
 1 (28-oz.) jar spaghetti sauce
^{1}/2 cup dry red wine
12 (^{1}/2-inch-thick) tomato slices

❶ Heat oven to 350°F.

❷ Sprinkle fillets with lemon-pepper seasoning. Roll each fillet around cheese stick; gently place inside pasta shell. Place shells, open side up, in 3-quart casserole.

❸ In large skillet, heat oil over medium-high heat until hot. Add mushrooms, bell pepper and garlic; sauté 2 to 3 minutes. Add spaghetti sauce and wine; bring to a boil. Pour sauce over shells. Cover casserole.

❹ Bake 15 to 20 minutes until thoroughly cooked. Top each shell with tomato slice.

4 servings.
Preparation time: 20 minutes. Ready to serve: 50 minutes.
Per serving: 555 calories, 17 g total fat (4 g saturated fat), 90 mg cholesterol, 1900 mg sodium, 6.5 g fiber.

CATFISH AND SHRIMP OVER GRITS

I pledge that this recipe will make you a lover of grits and catfish for breakfast, lunch or dinner!

1	tablespoon vegetable oil
1/2	cup all-purpose flour
1	tablespoon Cajun seasoning
3	cups catfish fillet pieces (2x2x1/2-inch)
1	tablespoon butter
2	cups sliced fresh mushrooms (1/4 inch thick)
1/4	cup chopped scallions (1/4-inch-thick rounds)
1	tablespoon chopped fresh tarragon
2	cups shelled, deveined uncooked jumbo shrimp
1/2	teaspoon salt
1/4	teaspoon freshly ground pepper
1	tablespoon balsamic vinegar
1	teaspoon Worcestershire sauce
4	cups *Grits Supreme* (page 168)

❶ In large skillet, heat oil over medium-high heat until hot.

❷ In shallow bowl, combine flour and Cajun seasoning. Dredge fillets in Cajun flour, shaking off excess. Place fillets in skillet; add butter. Cook fillets until golden and they flake easily with a fork. Turn fillets; arrange on one side of skillet.

❸ Add mushrooms, scallions and tarragon to skillet; sauté until mushrooms and scallions are tender. Add 1 teaspoon of the Cajun flour to make slightly thick sauce; stir to combine. Add shrimp, salt, pepper, vinegar and Worcestershire sauce; bring to a boil. Remove from heat; cover and let stand 5 minutes to steep or until shrimp turn pink.

❹ Place large serving of Grits Supreme in center of clean plate; make indentation in center of each. Top each with catfish, vegetables and shrimp sauce.

4 servings.

Preparation time: 15 minutes. Ready to serve: 30 minutes.

Per serving: 435 calories, 9.5 g total fat (3 g saturated fat), 220 mg cholesterol, 1355 mg sodium, 1.5 g fiber.

CHEF'S NOTE:
- Catfish fillets should not be more than 1/2 inch thick. If they are too thick, slice them in half.

OYSTERS ON THE HALF SHELL WITH HONZA SAUCE

In Czech, Honza means "John." This is my favorite way to enjoy as many oysters as I can.

    1   (12-oz.) bottle Burgundy wine
    1   cup ketchup
  1/2   cup grated fresh horseradish
  1/2   cup chili sauce
  1/4   teaspoon freshly ground pepper
  1/4   teaspoon finely grated lemon peel
   24   oysters on the half shell
    1   lemon, quartered

❶ In large pot, bring wine to a fast boil over medium heat. Cook until wine is reduced by half.

❷ Place reduced wine in large bowl. Add ketchup, horseradish, pepper, chili sauce and lemon peel; stir well to combine. Cover with plastic wrap. Poke 6 to 8 holes in top to help cool and chill evenly. Refrigerate 12 hours.

❸ Open oysters and place on well-chilled, rock salt-covered platter. Discard any unopened oysters. Serve sauce in chilled sauce bowl with lemon wedges.

4 to 6 servings.

Preparation time: 20 minutes. Ready to serve: 12 hours.

Per serving: 170 calories, 2.5 g total fat (0 g saturated fat), 46.5 mg cholesterol, 1290 mg sodium, 2 g fiber.

CHEF'S NOTES:
- Always make sure oysters are fresh. Open them as close to serving time as possible.
- For a smoother flavor, substitute Chianti for the Burgundy wine.

BASS AND WATER CHESTNUT STRUDEL

This is an excellent recipe for strong-flavored or oily fish. Substitute olive or peanut oil for the sesame oil if you wish.

¼ cup sesame oil	1 tablespoon finely minced fresh ginger
1 cup fresh wild mushrooms, cut into matchstick-size pieces	2 cups bass fillets, cut into 1-inch strips
½ cup zucchini, cut into matchstick-size pieces	½ cup sliced water chestnuts, drained
½ cup summer squash, cut into matchstick-size pieces	1 bunch chopped fresh cilantro
½ cup carrots, cut into matchstick-size pieces	2 teaspoons low-sodium soy sauce
½ cup red bell peppers, cut into matchstick-size pieces	⅛ teaspoon freshly ground pepper
½ cup green onions, cut into matchstick-size pieces	8 sheets *Phyllo Dough* (page 171)
	½ cup *Clarified Butter* (page 167)
	¼ cup *Egg Wash* (page 163)

❶ In large skillet, heat oil over medium-high heat until hot. Add mushrooms, zucchini, summer squash, carrots, bell peppers, onions and ginger; sauté 2 minutes or until onion is transparent and tender. Stir in fish, water chestnuts, cilantro, soy sauce and pepper. Cook until thoroughly heated and fish flakes easily with a fork. Remove skillet from heat; cover and let stand 5 minutes. Pour into colander to drain and cool.

❷ Brush each sheet of Phyllo Dough with Clarified Butter, building an 8-layer crust. Spread chilled fish mixture evenly over dough, leaving 1-inch strip per side and 2-inch strip on bottom free of filling. Lightly brush side and bottom strips with Egg Wash. Fold side strips over filling. Starting at top, roll up dough, jelly-roll fashion, towards bottom strip. Seal edge.

❸ Heat oven to 350°F. Line 15x10x1-inch pan with aluminum foil. Place strudel, seam side down, in pan. Lightly brush top of strudel with thin coat of Egg Wash. With knife, pierce strudel 4 times for steam to escape. Bake 25 minutes. Cut into 4 diagonal pieces. Place on warm serving plate. Serve with your favorite sauces.

4 servings.

Preparation time: 45 minutes. Ready to serve: 1 hour, 30 minutes.

Per serving: 820 calories, 50 g total fat (20 g saturated fat), 140 mg cholesterol, 635 mg sodium, 4.5 g fiber.

CHEF'S NOTE:
• To reheat, microwave strudel for 20 to 30 seconds.

SKILLET POACHED EGGS AND TROUT FILLETS IN TOMATO SALSA

This Tex-Mex breakfast is great for brunch too.

2	tablespoons olive oil
1	large red bell pepper, diced (1/4 inch thick)
1/2	cup diced white onions (1/4 inch thick)
2	garlic cloves, finely diced
1 1/2	cups tomato salsa
1/2	cup red wine
1/3	cup coarsely chopped fresh cilantro
1/8	teaspoon freshly ground pepper
4	(4- to 6-oz.) trout fillets, skins on
8	large eggs
4	(10-inch) soft tortillas

❶ In large skillet, heat olive oil over medium-high heat. Add bell pepper, onion and garlic; sauté until onions are transparent and tender. Add salsa, wine, cilantro and pepper; bring to a boil.

❷ Arrange trout fillets around edge of skillet. Arrange eggs in center of skillet. Reduce heat to medium; simmer 5 minutes. Remove from heat; cover 2 to 3 minutes or until fillets flake easily with a fork and eggs are cooked to desired doneness.

❸ Place tortillas on plates. With large spoon, remove fish, eggs and sauce from skillet; place on tortillas.

4 servings.

Preparation time: 15 minutes. Ready to serve: 40 minutes.

Per serving: 635 calories, 29 g total fat (6 g saturated fat), 490 mg cholesterol, 755 mg sodium, 5 g fiber.

CHEF'S NOTES:
- Any thin boneless fish fillets will work in this recipe.
- The trout fillets will cook very quickly.
- I like to add a little sour cream to this dish.
- The tortilla is not only excellent with fish, it covers the plate and helps cut down on dishwashing effort.

SOUPS & CHOWDERS

Of course, fish and seafood are the centers of the chowder universe. But soup benefits from the taste of finned and shelled creatures too. Here are the ideas you need on both fronts.

Fish and Shrimp Gumbo, page 53

ISH BISQUE

This is a rich soup made from thickened vegetables and fish steaks.

4 lb. fish bones, skin on, heads on
2 cups Granny Smith apples, cut into 1-inch pieces
1 cup each diced onions, celery (1/2 inch thick)
1 cup diced carrots (1/2-inch-thick rounds)
6 garlic cloves, minced
2 cups dry white wine
1 gallon cold water
1 cup tomato puree
1/2 cup *Roux* (page 169)
2 cups heavy cream
1/8 teaspoon salt
1/8 teaspoon freshly ground pepper
1 tablespoon finely minced fresh cilantro
3 cups diced boneless skinless fish fillets (1/2 inch thick)
Unsweetened whipped cream

> **CHEF'S NOTES:**
> - Use caution to avoid scorching soup.
> - Fish bones can be frozen for future use.
> - If soup is too thin, remove 2 cups liquid and place in blender; add 1/2 cup Roux and puree. Return to soup; simmer an additional 5 minutes over low heat.

❶ Place fish bones on cheesecloth. Tie to form bag. Place bag in large pot. Add apples, onions, celery, carrots, 4 of the garlic cloves, wine and water. Reduce heat to medium; simmer 1 hour.

❷ Remove bag, allowing liquid to drain into pot. Strain all liquid into clean, large pot. While vegetables are hot, puree in blender. Return pot to heat; bring to a slow boil to reduce liquid by half. Strain again; return liquid to pot. Boil until 1-quart liquid remains.

❸ When stock has reduced, stir in tomato puree. Whisk Roux into soup through strainer to keep soup from lumping. Let simmer 10 minutes.

❹ In medium bowl, combine cream and 1 cup hot liquid; whisk until smooth. Add mixture to soup; whisk until smooth. Add vegetable puree. If soup is too thick, add a little warm milk.

❺ Season soup with salt and pepper. Add fish; simmer 3 minutes until fish flakes easily with a fork. Cover; remove from heat. Let set 5 minutes. Serve in warm soup bowls. Top with large dollop of whipped cream.

4 servings.

Preparation time: 20 minutes. Ready to serve: 4 hours.

Per serving: 770 calories, 54 g total fat (32.5 g saturated fat), 240 mg cholesterol, 590 mg sodium, 5 g fiber.

$\mathcal{S}$HRIMP STEW

This shrimp stew is modeled after a hot savory stew from the coast of Brazil.

1/4 cup peanut oil
20 shelled, deveined uncooked jumbo shrimp
2 cups diced white onions (1/4 inch thick)
1 green bell pepper, diced (1/2 inch thick)
1 red bell pepper, diced (1/2 inch thick)
2 cups chopped tomatoes (1/2 inch thick)
1 cup piña colada mix
4 scallions, sliced (1/4 inch thick)
1/2 teaspoon ground coriander
1/4 teaspoon hot red pepper sauce
3 tablespoon minced fresh cilantro
1/2 teaspoon salt
1/4 teaspoon freshly ground pepper
1 recipe *Rice Pilaf* (page 165)

> **CHEF'S NOTES:**
> • This is a national dish from Brazil.
> • You can also make this recipe with fish or chicken.
> • For orange color and flavor, add 6 strands of saffron to the olive oil.
> • Mashed sweet potatoes make a colorful and delicious side dish.

❶ In large skillet, heat oil over medium-high heat until hot. Add shrimp; sauté 30 seconds on each side. Add onions and bell peppers; sauté until onions are transparent and tender. Stir in tomatoes, piña colada mix, scallions, coriander and hot red pepper sauce; mix well. Reduce heat to low; cover and simmer 10 minutes until shrimp turn pink.

❷ Add cilantro, salt and pepper; mix well. Pour mixture into heated soup tureen. Serve over Rice Pilaf.

4 servings.
Preparation time: 15 minutes. Ready to serve: 30 minutes.

Per serving: 525 calories, 21 g total fat (6.5 g saturated fat), 115 mg cholesterol, 630 mg sodium, 4.5 g fiber.

LEMON EGG DROP AND GINGER FISH SOUP

This recipe is quick to make and offers a snappy, tangy flavor from the fresh ginger and Szechuan peppercorns.

- 3 cups *Chicken Stock* (page 164)
- 1 (8-oz.) can clam broth
- 1/2 cup dry white wine
- 1 tablespoon diced fresh ginger
- 2 garlic cloves, finely minced
- 2 cups sliced fresh mushrooms (1/4 inch thick)
- 1/2 cup sliced green onions (1/4 inch thick)
- 2 teaspoons freshly grated lemon peel
- 6 Szechuan peppercorns
- 3 eggs
- 1 tablespoon low-sodium soy sauce
- 3 cups diced boneless skinless fish fillets (1/2 inch thick)
- 2 cups fresh spinach

❶ In large pot, combine Chicken Stock, clam broth, wine, ginger and garlic. Bring to a full boil over medium-high heat. Boil vigorously 5 minutes. Reduce heat to medium. Add mushrooms, onions, lemon peel and peppercorns; simmer 10 minutes.

❷ Break eggs into medium bowl. Add soy sauce; whisk until smooth.

❸ Bring soup back to a boil. Add eggs through colander while stirring broth. Remove from heat. Add diced fillets and spinach; cover and let steep 5 minutes or until fillets flake easily with a fork. Serve in large soup platters.

4 to 6 servings.

Preparation time: 45 minutes. Ready to serve: 2 hours, 30 minutes.

Per serving: 230 calories, 6.5 g total fat (2 g saturated fat), 230 mg cholesterol, 555 mg sodium, 2 g fiber.

CHEF'S NOTES:
- This is a great soup for the kids.
- Panfish fillets are the best fish choice for this recipe.
- If you don't have Szechuan peppercorns, use black or white peppercorns.
- You can also add a few shrimp, scallops or oysters with the fillets.
- Adding eggs through a strainer, with the liquid moving, keeps the eggs from forming large lumps. Eggs should look wispy in the soup.

SHELLFISH SOUP

This is a cornucopia of great shellfish flavors. This recipe is perfect for family holidays.

2 tablespoons olive oil	1 cup small butter beans
1 cup diced red onions (½ inch thick)	1 cup diced green pear (¼ inch thick)
1 cup each sliced celery, fennel (¼ inch thick)	½ cup dry white wine
1 cup diced carrots (¼ inch thick)	4 cups littleneck clams
3 garlic cloves, finely minced	4 cups mussels, beards removed or debearded
1½ tablespoons all-purpose flour	16 shelled, deveined uncooked jumbo shrimp
1 (28-oz.) can diced tomatoes, juice reserved	1 large baguette, cut into 1-inch-thick slices
2 (8-oz.) cans clam broth	4 tablespoons butter
1 teaspoon each salt, chili powder	8 (1-oz.) slices Swiss cheese
1 teaspoon Worcestershire sauce	
1 cup unpeeled diced red potato (½ inch thick)	

1 In large pot, heat oil over medium-high heat until hot. Add onions, celery, carrots, fennel and garlic; sauté until onions are transparent and tender. Stir in flour; cook 2 minutes, stirring with wooden spoon to keep flour from scorching.

2 Add tomatoes with juice, clam broth, salt, chili powder and Worcestershire sauce,; bring to a simmer. Do not boil. Add potatoes; cook an additional 20 minutes.

3 Add butter beans, pears and wine; simmer 5 minutes. Vegetables are done when firm. Add clams, mussels and shrimp. Reduce heat to low; cover and simmer 10 minutes. Remove from heat; cover and let stand 10 minutes to steep or until shellfish are thoroughly cooked.

4 Heat oven to 375°F. Spray 15x10x1-inch pan with nonstick cooking spray. Brush each slice baguette with butter; top each with 1 slice cheese. Bake until cheese is melted and golden brown. Place 1 to 2 pieces in each soup platter. Ladle shellfish, vegetables and broth over top.

4 servings.

Preparation time: 30 minutes.
Ready to serve: 1 hour, 55 minutes.

Per serving: 920 calories, 26 g total fat (10 g saturated fat), 225 mg cholesterol, 2470 mg sodium, 12.5 g fiber

---

CHEF'S NOTE:
- Wash all the shellfish in clean cold water, and clean each one individually with a vegetable brush.

$\mathcal{S}$KILLET FISH SOUP

When short on time and long on appetite, make this recipe.

6 thick-slices uncooked bacon, diced (1/2 inch thick)
1 cup diced onions (1/2 inch thick)
1 cup diced carrots (1/2 inch thick)
1 cup diced celery (1/2 inch thick)
1 cup diced red bell peppers (1/2 inch thick)
1 tablespoon all-purpose flour
3 cups water
1 cup ketchup
1 (12-oz.) can beer
2 russet potatoes, unpeeled, diced (1/2 inch thick)
1 teaspoon dried thyme
1 teaspoon dried dill
1 teaspoon salt
1/8 teaspoon freshly ground pepper
3 cups diced boneless fish fillets (1/2 inch thick)

> **CHEF'S NOTE:**
> • Ketchup has vinegar and spices and if not over used, it adds a nice flavor to the soup.

❶ In large saucepan, cook bacon over medium heat until crisp. Add onions, carrots, celery and bell peppers; sauté until onions are transparent and tender. Add flour; stir with wooden spoon to keep flour from burning and to pick up bacon drippings. Cook 3 minutes.

❷ Add water, ketchup, beer, tomatoes, thyme, dill, salt and pepper to saucepan. Simmer 20 minutes.

❸ Add fish to soup; simmer 5 minutes or until fish flakes easily with a fork. Remove from heat; cover and stand 5 minutes before serving.

8 servings.

Preparation time: 20 minutes.
Ready to serve: 1 hour.

Per serving: 330 calories, 19 g total fat (7 g saturated fat),
55 mg cholesterol, 875 mg sodium, 2.5 g fiber.

TOMATO, ARTICHOKE HEART AND WHITE BEAN FISH SOUP

This soup is almost too healthy and good for you to eat.

1 tablespoon olive oil
1 cup diced celery (1/2 inch thick)
8 whole shallots
2 whole garlic cloves
1 cup dry white beans
4 cups stewed whole tomatoes, liquid reserved
4 cups *Chicken Stock* (page 164)
1 cup dry red wine
2 (14-oz.) cans artichoke hearts, drained, quartered

2 tablespoons coarsely chopped fresh cilantro
2 tablespoons balsamic vinegar
3 cups diced boneless skinless fish fillets (1/2 inch thick)
1 teaspoon kosher (coarse) salt
1/4 teaspoon freshly ground pepper
1/2 cup (2 oz.) freshly grated Parmesan cheese

❶ In large pot, heat olive oil over medium-high heat until hot. Add celery, shallots and garlic; sauté until garlic turns golden brown. Gently stir in dried beans, being careful not to break up whole shallots. Sauté until beans are hot.

❷ Add tomatoes with juice, Chicken Stock and wine; mix well. Reduce heat to medium; simmer, uncovered, about 45 minutes or until beans are tender. If liquid starts to evaporate, add warm water to keep liquid level.

❸ Gently stir in artichoke hearts, cilantro and balsamic vinegar. Reduce heat to low. Add diced fillets; cover and simmer 5 minutes until fillets flake easily with a fork.

❹ Stir in salt and pepper. Serve in soup mugs. Top with freshly grated Parmesan cheese.

8 servings.

Preparation time: 15 minutes. Ready to serve: 2 hours.

Per serving: 290 calories, 5.5 g total fat (2 g saturated fat), 40 mg cholesterol, 100 mg sodium, 9.5 g fiber.

CHEF'S NOTES:

• Black beans can be used in this recipe.

• For added color: Just before serving add 1 tablespoon cooked sweet peas in the bottom of each soup mug.

• Shellfish and shrimp can be added with the fish fillets.

• Light-colored olive oil has less flavor than dark-colored olive oil.

• If soup needs additional broth, add hot Chicken Stock to achieve desired consistency.

EW ENGLAND CLAM CHOWDER

There are as many recipes for this traditional white clam chowder as there are families in New England.

4	cups cold water
1	cup dry white wine
8	black peppercorns
2	garlic cloves
15 to 20	chowder clams in shell
1	cup diced salt pork (1/4 inch thick)
1	tablespoon butter
1	cup each diced white onions, celery (1/4 inch thick)
1/3	cup all-purpose flour
2 1/2	cups diced russet potatoes (1/2 inch thick)
1	tablespoon chopped fresh thyme
2	teaspoons Worcestershire sauce
3	cups half-and-half

CHEF'S NOTES:

- For a richer soup, use light cream instead of half-and-half.
- Use fresh thyme.
- I sometimes add 1 cup lump crabmeat or shrimp pieces with chopped clams.
- For thicker soup, increase flour from 1/3 to 1/2 cup.
- To reheat chowder, use a heavy soup pot and heat on low to medium heat, stirring frequently and gently.
- Place any leftover chowder in a covered glass or stainless steel bowl and refrigerate as soon as you're done serving it.

❶ In large pot, combine water, wine, peppercorns and garlic. Bring to a rapid boil over medium-high heat. Gently add clams; cover and steam 5 minutes. When shells have opened, place clams in large bowl. Discard clams that do not open.

❷ Strain broth into separate containers. Set broth aside. Rinse pot with cold water; return to medium heat. Add salt pork and butter; cook until salt pork is light brown, stirring frequently with wooden spoon to keep pork from sticking to bottom.

❸ Add onions and celery; sauté until onions are transparent and tender. Stir in flour with wooden spoon until well combined. Reduce heat to low; cook 4 minutes, stirring frequently. Slowly stir in reserved broth, potatoes, thyme and Worcestershire sauce. Simmer 20 minutes or until potatoes are just tender.

❹ In medium bowl, combine half-and half with several ladles of hot stock from pot. Slowly add half-and-half mixture to soup; stir to combine. Cut clams in pieces; add to pot. Simmer 10 minutes. Adjust seasoning and serve.

4 servings.

Preparation time: 30 minutes. Ready to serve: 1 hour, 30 minutes.

Per serving: 670 calories, 47 g total fat (23 g saturated fat), 115 mg cholesterol, 570 mg sodium, 3.5 g fiber.

CHUNKY FISH VEGETABLE SOUP

This is a hardy lunch soup to feed family and friends!

1 tablespoon olive oil
3 ribs celery, diced (1/2 inch thick)
2 carrots, diced (1/2 inch thick)
1 jumbo white onion, diced (1/2 inch thick)
4 cups *Chicken Stock* (page 164)
1 cup dry white wine
1 (15-oz.) can whole tomatoes, juice reserved
1 cup diced zucchini (1/2 inch thick)
2 russet potatoes, diced (1/2 inch thick)
1 red bell pepper, diced (1/2 inch thick)
1 tablespoon chopped fresh basil
1 teaspoon salt
1 teaspoon whole thyme
1/4 teaspoon freshly ground pepper
2 bay leaves
4 (1-lb.) boneless skinless fish fillets

❶ In medium pot, heat olive oil over medium-high heat until hot. Add celery, carrots and onion; sauté until onion is transparent and tender. Add Chicken Stock, wine, tomatoes, zucchini, potatoes, bell pepper, basil, salt, thyme, pepper and bay leaves; simmer 30 minutes.

❷ Add fillets; simmer an additional 2 minutes or until they flake easily with a fork. Remove and discard bay leaves. Serve soup in bowls topped with fillets.

8 servings.

Preparation time: 30 minutes. Ready to serve: 1 hour, 20 minutes.

Per serving: 140 calories, 3 g total fat (1 g saturated fat), 30 mg cholesterol, 475 mg sodium, 2.5 g fiber.

FISH AND SHRIMP GUMBO

The soup recipe tastes better every day you keep it. It's important to reheat the soup each time. Add and simmer fresh fillets.

1 lb. thick-sliced uncooked bacon, diced (1/4 inch thick)

1 cup all-purpose flour

2 cups sliced white onions (1/4 inch thick)

2 cups each diced celery, diced red and green bell peppers

3 garlic cloves, minced

1 cup sliced green onions (1/4 inch thick)

4 (8-oz.) cans clam juice

3 cups diced stewed tomatoes, juice reserved

2 cups each sliced fresh mushrooms, okra (1/4 inch thick)

1/4 cup Worcestershire sauce

2 jalapeño chiles, seeded, diced (1/4 inch thick)

1 tablespoon each chopped fresh thyme, basil, oregano

2 teaspoons filé powder

1 teaspoon salt

1/2 teaspoon freshly ground pepper

4 cups *Chicken Stock* (page 164)

4 smoked pork chops

3 cups diced catfish fillets (1 1/2 to 2 inch pieces)

3 cups popcorn shrimp

4 cups *Long-Grain White Rice* (page 168)

❶ In large skillet, cook bacon over medium heat until crisp. Remove bacon from skillet; place in medium bowl.

❷ Reduce heat to low. Add flour to skillet with bacon drippings; stir with wooden spoon 10 minutes or until flour and fat are browned. Do not burn as this will give the flour a bitter flavor. Add onions, celery, bell peppers and garlic; stir to combine. Increase heat to medium; cook 5 minutes.

❸ Stir in clam juice, tomatoes with juice, mushrooms, okra, Worcestershire sauce, chiles, thyme, basil, oregano, filé powder, salt, pepper and cooked bacon. Add Chicken Stock and smoked pork chops. Reduce heat to low; simmer 1 hour, being careful not to boil. Stir very gently from time to time to keep ingredients from sticking.

❹ Just before serving, add diced fish and shrimp to soup. Cover; simmer 5 minutes until fillets flake easily with a fork. Remove from heat; let stand an additional 5 minutes to steep. In large soup platters, combine 1/2 cup Long-Grain White Rice with fish, shrimp, vegetables, pork chops and broth.

8 servings.

Preparation time: 45 minutes. Ready to serve: 2 hours, 30 minutes.

Per serving: 895 calories, 54.5 g total fat (20.5 g saturated fat), 215 mg cholesterol, 2185 mg sodium, 5 g fiber.

MANHATTAN CLAM CHOWDER

Sometimes called Red Clam Chowder because of the tomatoes, this soup must be thick and is always best made from freshly steamed chowder clams.

4	cups cold water
1	cup dry red wine
8	black peppercorns
2	garlic cloves
18 to 20	chowder clams in shells
1	cup diced salt pork (1/4 inch thick)
1	tablespoon olive oil
1	cup sliced celery (1/2 inch thick)
1	cup each diced carrots, red onions (1/2 inch thick)
1/4	cup all-purpose flour
1	cup diced red bell peppers (1/2 inch thick)
2	tablespoons chopped fresh thyme
1	teaspoon Worcestershire sauce
4	drops hot red pepper sauce
2	(14-oz.) cans diced tomatoes, juice reserved
2	cups diced unpeeled red potatoes (1/2 inch thick)

CHEF'S NOTES:

- If you are not a red wine fan, add white wine or no wine at all. Replace wine volume with extra water.
- You can add shrimp in the shell or crabmeat to this recipe, at the last stage, with the diced clam pieces.

❶ In large pot combine water, wine, peppercorns and garlic. Bring to a rapid boil over medium-high heat; boil 2 minutes. Gently add clams; cover and steam 5 minutes or until shells just begin to open. Place clams and liquid in large bowl to cool. Discard clams that do not open.

❷ Clean pot; return to burner over medium-high heat. Add pork and oil; cook until salt pork is light brown, stirring frequently with wooden spoon to keep pork from sticking to bottom. Stir in celery, carrots and onions; sauté until onions are transparent and tender. Stir in flour until well combined. Reduce heat to low; cook 2 minutes, stirring frequently. Add bell pepper, thyme, Worcestershire sauce and hot red pepper sauce; mix well.

❸ Strain broth through fine strainer into another pot. Add tomatoes with juice and potatoes, stirring well to combine. Increase heat to medium; simmer 30 minutes. Do not boil.

❹ Remove clams from shells; cut into 1/4-inch pieces. Remove and discard garlic and peppercorns. Add clams to pot; simmer 5 minutes. Adjust seasonings and serve.

4 servings.

Preparation time: 30 minutes. Ready to serve: 1 hour, 20 minutes.

Per serving: 480 calories, 27 g total fat (8.5 g saturated fat), 45x mg cholesterol, 805 mg sodium, 6.5 g fiber.

FISH CHILI

For this recipe, I prefer to use salmon, lake trout or firm saltwater fish, to keep pieces intact. Use a stronger flavored fish so it will not be overwhelmed by the chili powder.

1	tablespoon olive oil
1 1/2	cups chopped red onions (1/2 inch thick)
1	cup sliced celery (1/4 inch thick)
2	garlic cloves, finely minced
3	cups canned diced tomatoes, juice reserved
1	cup dry red wine
1	can butter beans, drained
1	can chili beans
4	cups diced fish fillets (1/2 inch thick)
2	tablespoons chili powder
1	tablespoon finely chopped fresh cilantro
1	teaspoon salt
1/2	teaspoon cumin
1/2	teaspoon allspice
1/4	teaspoon cinnamon
1/4	teaspoon freshly ground pepper
2	jalapeño chiles, stem removed, seeded, diced (1/4 inch thick)

CHEF'S NOTES:

- For garnish, mix 1 cup sour cream with 2 teaspoons chili powder. Spoon a dollop on top of each serving of the chili.
- Shredded farmer cheese sprinkled on top of the sour cream adds a nice touch.
- If you feel adventuresome, add a few shrimp or scallops to the chili.

❶ In large pot, heat oil over medium-high heat until hot. Add onions, garlic and celery; sauté until onions are transparent and tender. Add tomatoes with juice, wine, butter beans, chili beans, chiles, chili powder, cilantro, salt, cumin, allspice, cinnamon and pepper. Reduce heat to low; simmer 30 minutes, stirring frequently with wooden spoon to avoid scorching.

❷ Add fish to chili; cover and cook 5 minutes until they flake easily with a fork. Gently ladle chili into bowls, being careful to not break up fish.

8 servings.

Preparation time: 15 minutes. Ready to serve: 1 hour.

Per serving: 210 calories, 3.5 g total fat (1 g saturated fat), 45 mg cholesterol, 760 mg sodium, 6.5 g fiber.

SALADS & SANDWICHES

Fish and seafood's gentle tastes
and light textures blend
perfectly with salad and
sandwich ideas. A little out of
the ordinary, yes. But definitely
delightful!

*Grilled Fruit Salad with Seared Scallops and
Shrimp, page 67*

FISH BLT TRIPLE DECKERS

This is a whopper to see, but even more fun to eat.

2   tablespoons olive oil
4   (4- to 6-oz.) boneless skinless fish fillets
2   avocados, cut into 1/2-inch slices
1   tablespoon fresh lemon juice
1   cup *Tartar Sauce* (page 162)
1   tablespoon drained capers
2   large ripe large fresh tomatoes, sliced (1/2 inch thick)
1   teaspoon kosher (coarse) salt
1/8   teaspoon freshly ground pepper
12   slices sourdough bread
1   head leaf lettuce
8   thick slices bacon, cooked

❶ In large skillet, heat oil over medium-high heat until hot. Add fillets; fry until golden brown and they flake easily with a fork.

❷ In medium bowl, combine avocados with lemon juice. Add Tartar Sauce and capers; mix well. Stir in salt and pepper.

❸ Toast bread until golden brown. Place toasted bread on clean kitchen towel in lines 3 slices tall.

❹ To make each triple decker sandwich, spread each bread slice with generous amount of Tartar Sauce mixture. On each of 2 slices, place 1 lettuce leaf. Top 1 lettuce leaf with 2 tomato slices and 2 slices of bacon. Top other lettuce leaf with fish.

❺ Now the fun part: Top bacon/lettuce/tomato piece with sauce-spread bread slice, sauce side down. Spread dry side of slice with more Tartar Sauce mixture; top with lettuce leaf. Turn fish/avocado piece over top of slice to make third deck. Secure with 2 long wooden toothpicks; cut sandwich in half. Serve with kosher dill pickles.

4 servings.

Preparation time: 20 minutes. Ready to serve: 30 minutes.

Per serving: 990 calories, 70 g total fat (13 g saturated fat), 110 mg cholesterol, 1755 mg sodium, 11 g fiber.

CHEF'S NOTES:
• To keep all 3 decks together, spread sauce on both sides of the middle bread slice.
• You can use crisp iceberg lettuce in place of the leaf lettuce.
• If you are not a bacon lover, use turkey or corned beef instead.

SMOKED FISH, PEAR, STILTON AND PECAN SALAD

Throw a little caution to the wind. Be wild and try new flavors!

- 2 Bartlett pears, cored, each cut into 16 slices
- 1/2 cup fresh orange juice
- 1/2 cup raspberry vinaigrette
- 1 cup diced fennel root (1/4 inch thick)
- 1/2 cup pecans, halved
- 1 1/2 teaspoons packed brown sugar
- 1/4 teaspoon Spanish paprika
- 2 lb. smoked fish
- 1/2 cup (2 oz.) crumbled Stilton cheese
- 8 cups fresh assorted greens

> **CHEF'S NOTES:**
> - All smoked fish and gravlax work in this recipe.
> - Substitute yellow apples for the pears if you wish.

❶ In medium bowl, combine pear slices, orange juice and vinaigrette; mix well. In small bowl, combine fennel and pecans; mix well. In another small bowl, combine brown sugar and paprika; mix well.

❷ With fork, remove smoked fish from skin, picking out all small bones; place in large bowl. Add cheese and fennel with pecans; toss to mix well.

❸ Arrange greens evenly in 4 chilled salad bowls. Spoon fish mixture evenly onto lettuce. Decorate each salad with 8 pear slices. Sprinkle brown sugar mixture evenly over pears. Strain orange-raspberry vinaigrette into dressing boat; serve with salads.

4 (2-cup) servings.

Preparation time: 15 minutes. Ready to serve: 20 minutes.

Per serving: 440 calories, 27 g total fat (6 g saturated fat), 70 mg cholesterol, 1005 mg sodium, 5 g fiber

POPEYE FISH SANDWICH

Tough guys or gals also toss in one or two of their favorite hot peppers!

4   (6-oz.) boneless fish steaks
1   cup herbed vinegar and oil dressing
1   large red onion, cut into 1/4-inch-thick rings
2   tablespoons vegetable oil
4   French or Italian hard rolls, halved
1/3 cup honey mustard
4   cups fresh spinach, stems removed
4   (1-oz.) slices dill Havarti cheese
4   slices pineapple

❶ In large resealable plastic bag, combine steaks and dressing; seal bag. Shake to evenly coat. Refrigerate 1 hour.

❷ Place 3 layers of paper towels on work surface. Place onion slices on paper towel; top with another 3 layers of paper towels. With palm of hand, firmly press on onion slices to squeeze out juice. Turn onion slices over and repeat.

❸ In large skillet, heat oil over medium-high heat until hot. Remove steaks from dressing; discard dressing. Add steaks to skillet; fry until golden brown on each side and flaky.

❹ Spread cut sides of roll with honey mustard. On top half of each roll, place 1 cup spinach, 1 slice cheese and onion slices. On bottom half place 1 steak and pineapple slice. Assemble sandwiches.

4 servings.

Preparation time: 15 minutes.
Ready to serve: 20 minutes.

Per serving: 600 calories, 30 g total fat (9 g saturated fat), 120 mg cholesterol, 940 mg sodium, 4.5 g fiber.

FISH SALAD TULIPS

This is a show stopper for a spring lunch or brunch!

    2   cups chopped boneless skinless fish fillets
    4   cups *Chicken Stock* (page 164)
  1/2   cup mayonnaise
  1/4   cup sour cream
    2   teaspoons sugar
    1   teaspoon chopped fresh dill
    1   teaspoon fresh lemon juice
    1   teaspoon Worcestershire sauce
  1/8   teaspoon salt
  1/8   teaspoon ground white pepper
    2   hard-cooked eggs, chopped
  1/2   cup diced celery (1/4 inch thick)
   12   tulips
    1   head leaf lettuce

❶ In large pot, poach fillets in Chicken Stock 8 minutes or until they flake easily with a fork; drain. Refrigerate 1 hour.

❷ In medium bowl, combine mayonnaise, sour cream, sugar, dill, lemon juice, Worcestershire sauce, salt and pepper; mix well. Add eggs, celery and poached fillets. Stir gently to combine.

❸ Remove pistils and stems from tulips. Place tulips in cold, salted water. Let stand 5 minutes. Remove tulips; gently shake dry. On each of 4 plates, place 1/4 head of lettuce. Place 3 tulips over lettuce on each. Fill each tulip with fish salad. Serve with sweet pickles, slices of melon and soft rolls, if desired.

4 servings.

Preparation time: 30 minutes. Ready to serve: 30 minutes.

Per serving: 375 calories, 30 g total fat (6 g saturated fat), 180 mg cholesterol, 380 mg sodium, 2.5 g fiber.

CHEF'S NOTES:
- Prior to dicing celery, peel stalks with potato peeler to remove celery strings.
- If you have leftover fried or baked fish, remove excess breading.

GRILLED FISH & VEGETABLE GRINDERS

Use your imagination when building this grinder (sandwich). Incorporate fresh grilled fruits or vegetables, capers or hot peppers to name a few. Good luck — this is a two-handed grinder.

1 cup mayonnaise	2 large ripe tomatoes, sliced (1/2 inch thick)
1 tablespoon *Chef John's Fish Rub* (page 162)	2 large red bell peppers, seeded, cut into 3 wedges
1 tablespoon fresh lemon juice	1 cup *Tartar Sauce* (page 162)
1 teaspoon spicy mustard	1 teaspoon garlic salt
4 (6- to 8-oz.) boneless fish steaks	1/4 teaspoon freshly ground pepper
2/3 cup barbecue sauce	1 cup (4 oz.) shredded Muenster cheese
1/2 cup vegetable oil	
3 large russet potatoes, sliced lengthwise (1/2 inch thick)	1 (12- to 14-inch) French or Italian loaf bread, halved lengthwise
3 large carrots, sliced lengthwise (1/4 inch thick)	1 head iceberg lettuce
2 large red onions, sliced (1/2 inch thick)	1 cup sliced ripe olives

❶ In large resealable plastic bag, combine mayonnaise, Chef John's Fish Rub, lemon juice and mustard; seal bag. Shake to combine. Add steaks; seal bag. Shake gently to coat steaks. Refrigerate 1 to 2 hours.

❷ Heat grill. Place barbecue sauce and oil in 9-inch cake pan; stir to mix. Dip bell peppers, carrots, onions and potatoes in barbecue-flavored oil; place on gas grill over medium heat or on charcoal grill 4 to 6 inches from medium coals. Remove fish from bag, leaving thick coat of mayonnaise mixture on steaks. Add to grill; cook vegetables and steaks until golden brown. Turn and grill until vegetables are tender and flaky in center.

❸ In large bowl, combine Tartar Sauce, garlic salt, pepper and cheese; mix well. Spread each half loaf with 1/2 cup of the Tartar Sauce mixture. Arrange bread halves on platter. Top bottom half with grilled potatoes. Brush with barbecue-flavored oil. Add bell pepper wedges, lettuce leaves, olives, steaks, tomatoes, onions and carrots. Brush with barbecue-flavored oil.

❹ Turn top half of loaf quickly onto bottom half. Cut into 4 slices. Secure each slice with long wooden toothpick.

4 servings.

Preparation time: 20 minutes. Ready to serve: 40 minutes.

Per serving: 1420 calories, 86 g total fat (17.5 g saturated fat), 160 mg cholesterol, 2090 mg sodium, 14 g fiber.

BEEFSTEAK TOMATO AND FISH CAESAR SALAD

A fun way to add color and flavor to your old favorite, Caesar Salad!

1/4 cup olive oil
4   small garlic cloves, minced
1/2 cup *Seasoned Flour* (page 170)
4   (6- to 8-oz.) boneless skinless fish fillets
4   yellow jalapeño chiles, halved lengthwise, stems removed, seeded
1 1/2 cups diced French bread (1/2 inch thick)
1   head romaine lettuce
3   ripe large beefsteak tomatoes, stems removed, cut into
      4 (1/2-inch-thick) slices
1/4 teaspoon freshly ground pepper
1/2 cup (2 oz.) freshly grated Parmesan cheese
2   tablespoons drained capers
1   tablespoon fresh lemon juice
2   cups *Easy Caesar Dressing* (page 166)

❶ In large skillet, heat oil and garlic over medium-high heat until hot. Place Seasoned Flour in 9-inch pie plate. Dredge fillets and chile halves in Seasoned Flour, shaking off excess. Add fillets and chiles to skillet; fry until golden brown on both sides and fillets flake easily with a fork. Place fillets and garlic on clean plate. Keep warm in oven at 250°F.

❷ Add bread to hot oil in skillet; sauté until golden brown, tossing to keep from sticking. Remove to paper-towel-lined bowl.

❸ On each of 4 chilled dinner plates, place 3 to 4 lettuce leaves. Top each with 3 tomato slices and 2 chile halves; sprinkle with pepper. Place fillets on top of tomato slices. Sprinkle cheese over fillets. Top cheese with capers. Sprinkle with fresh lemon juice. Serve with Easy Caesar Dressing.

4 servings.

Preparation time: 20 minutes. Ready to serve: 40 minutes.

Per serving: 1175 calories, 98 g total fat (16.5 g saturated fat), 115 mg cholesterol, 1605 mg sodium, 5.5 g fiber.

CHEF'S NOTES:
• Any trout or salmon fillet can be used in this recipe.
• I am an anchovy fan so I add 2 fillets per salad.
• The riper and bigger the tomato, the better. Yellow tomatoes are very good too.

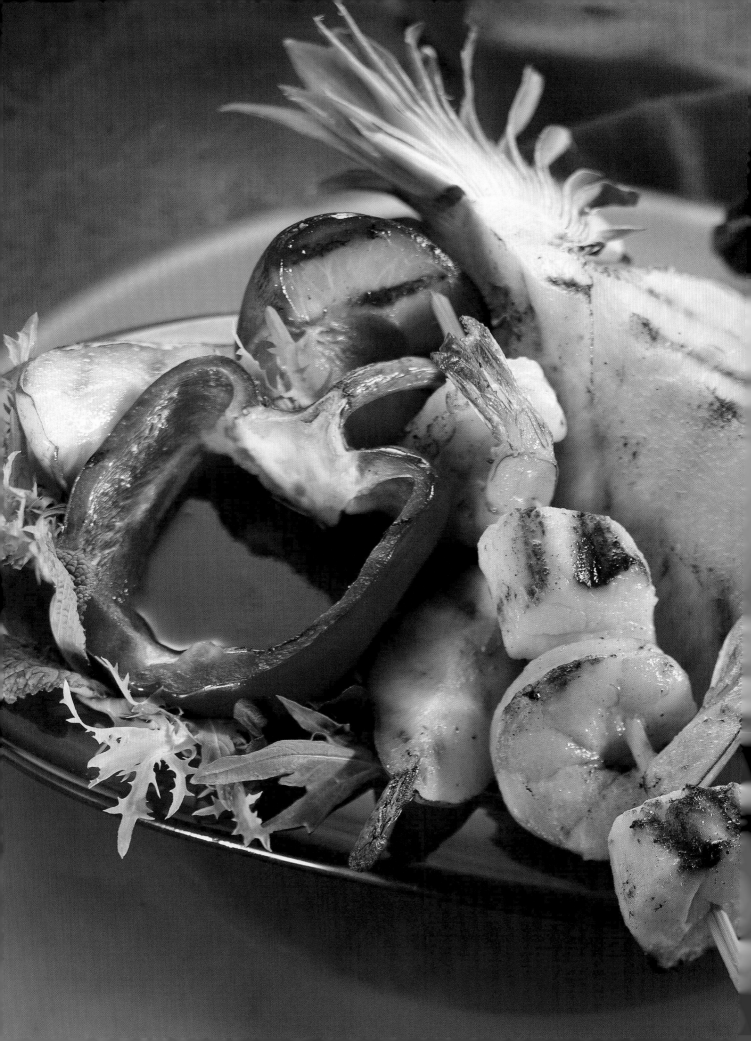

GRILLED FRUIT SALAD WITH SEARED SCALLOPS AND SHRIMP

I also serve this as a hot dinner salad, grilling the fruit and seafood at the same time and serving them on a bed of spinach leaves.

3/4 cup *Seasoned Flour* (page 170)
1 tablespoon nondairy coffee cream
1 teaspoon salt
1/4 teaspoon ground white pepper
1/2 cup barbecue sauce
1/2 cup *Melba Sauce* (page 170)
1 tablespoon balsamic vinegar
4 large plums, halved, pits removed
1 whole pineapple, quartered
2 Bartlett pears, cored, quartered
2 red bell peppers, halved lengthwise, seeds removed
1/4 cup olive oil
8 shelled, deveined uncooked jumbo shrimp, halved lengthwise, tails on
8 large sea scallops, halved across grain
8 cups mixed greens

> **CHEF'S NOTES:**
> • If you wish, use whole shrimp and scallops. Just grill on lower heat.

❶ In 9-inch pie plate, combine Seasoned Flour, creamer, salt and pepper. In blender, blend barbecue sauce, Melba Sauce and vinegar until smooth.

❷ Heat grill. With pastry brush coat plums, pears, pineapple and bell peppers on all sides with oil. Place on gas grill over medium heat or on charcoal grill 4 to 6 inches from grill. Cook until golden brown. Turn; cook other side. Place on clean platter; refrigerate.

❸ Dredge shrimp and scallop slices in Seasoned Flour mixture. Place 2 scallop pieces and 2 shrimp on each of 8 bamboo skewers. Brush with oil. Place on grill; cook 1 minute on each side until shrimp turn pink and scallops turn opaque. Place skewers on another clean platter; brush with barbecue sauce mixture. Refrigerate.

❹ Place 2 cups of the mixed greens in center of each plate. Top greens with equal amounts of fruit. Place 1 grilled pepper half in center of each; fill each pepper with 1/4 cup of the barbecue mixture. For each salad, place 2 skewers of grilled seafood on top of barbecue-filled pepper.

4 servings.

Preparation time: 30 minutes. Ready to serve: 45 minutes.

Per serving: 445 calories, 10 g total fat (1 g saturated fat), 50 mg cholesterol, 1180 mg sodium, 10 g fiber.

$\mathcal{F}$ISH BURGERS

This is a great alternative to meat burgers.

2	tablespoons *Clarified Butter* (page 167)
1	cup diced celery (1/4 inch thick)
1/2	cup diced scallions (1/4 inch thick)
1	tablespoon fresh thyme or 1 teaspoon dried
1	tablespoon horseradish, squeezed dry
1	teaspoon kosher (coarse) salt
1/4	teaspoon freshly ground pepper
2	teaspoons Worcestershire sauce
4	cups diced boneless fish fillets (1/4 inch thick)
2	eggs, beaten
1 to 1 1/2	cups *Fresh Bread Crumbs* (page 163)
1/2	cup *Seasoned Flour* (page 170)

> **CHEF'S NOTE:**
> • If the mix is too loose, the patties will flatten out during cooking. If the mix is too firm, the patties will crack and dry out.

❶ Heat oven to 350°F.

❷ In large skillet, melt 1 tablespoon of the Clarified Butter over medium-high heat. Add celery and scallions; sauté 1 to 2 minutes or until celery is transparent and tender. Place in large bowl; cool 10 minutes.

❸ Stir in thyme, horseradish, salt, pepper, Worcestershire sauce, fish and eggs, stirring gently to form paste. Sprinkle Fresh Bread Crumbs over top. Stir to make firm mixture. If mixture is too loose, add more bread crumbs a few at a time.

❹ Cover bottom of 9-inch pie plate with Seasoned Flour. To make each fish patty, fill coffee cup with mixture; press firmly. Remove patty from cup; roll in Seasoned Flour, forming desired shape. Place on plate; refrigerate until firm.

❺ In another large skillet, heat remaining 1 tablespoon butter to a fast bubble over medium-high heat. Gently add patties, being careful not to overcrowd. Cook until bottoms are golden brown. Turn with wide spatula; brown other side. Transfer patties to baking sheet; bake 10 minutes or until patties are thoroughly heated and fish is cooked. Serve on roll with your favorite cheese.

4 servings.

Preparation time: 20 minutes. Ready to serve: 40 minutes.

Per serving: 480 calories, 28 g total fat (5 g saturated fat), 210 mg cholesterol, 1150 mg sodium, 2 g fiber.

SHRIMP AND FISH BITE SANDWICH

The bite comes from the wasabi (Japanese horseradish). This recipe wants to make you bite back.

1	cup mayonnaise
1	cup sliced fresh ginger
2	tablespoons wasabi paste
1	teaspoon fresh lemon juice
1	teaspoon Worcestershire sauce
1/4	teaspoon celery salt
1/4	teaspoon dry mustard
1/8	teaspoon ground white pepper
1	teaspoon cornstarch
8	thick slices sourdough bread
8	shelled, deveined uncooked jumbo shrimp
4	(4-oz.) boneless fish steaks
8	lettuce leaves
1	lemon, quartered

CHEF'S NOTES:

- If you are a shrimp lover, omit fish and grill 4 to 6 shrimp per sandwich.
- If you prefer scallops, place 3 scallops on each skewer before grilling.
- The best of all worlds is to use boiled lobster tails split in half.
- Remember not to over cook the lobster on the grill.

❶ Heat grill.

❷ In medium bowl, whisk together mayonnaise, ginger, wasabi paste, lemon juice, Worcestershire sauce, celery salt, dry mustard and pepper. Sprinkle cornstarch over top; whisk until smooth.

❸ With brush, brush both sides of bread slices with mayonnaise mixture. Then, generously coat shrimp and steaks with mayonnaise mixture.

❹ Place steaks on gas grill over medium heat or on charcoal grill 4 to 6 inches from medium coals. Cook until golden brown on one side. Turn steaks; add shrimp to grill. Grill shrimp until they turn pink. Turn shrimp; add bread slices to grill. Cook until golden brown on both sides. Place grilled bread slices on large serving platter. Remove steaks from grill; place on large platter.

❺ Top 4 grilled slices of bread with generous amount of lettuce, 2 shrimp and 1 steak. On side of each sandwich, lean grilled bread slice. Serve with lemon wedges.

4 servings.

Preparation time: 10 minutes. Ready to serve: 30 minutes.

Per serving: 740 calories, 48 g total fat (7.5 g saturated fat), 135 mg cholesterol, 980 mg sodium, 4 g fiber.

SAUTÉ & PAN FRY

*Now we're getting into the
traditional realm of fish and
seafood dishes. These recipes are
anything but ordinary, though.*

Fish Stir-Fry, page 88

FISH BEURRE BLANC

Beurre Blanc means white butter, a classic French sauce.

  1 cup *Seasoned Flour* (page 170)
  4 (8-oz.) boneless skinless fish fillets
  1 tablespoon *Clarified Butter* (page 167)
  2 tablespoons chopped shallots
1 1/2 cups dry white wine
  1/4 teaspoon salt
  1/8 teaspoon ground white pepper
  8 slices lemon

❶ Heat oven to 350°F.

❷ Place Seasoned Flour in 9-inch pie plate. Dredge fillets in Seasoned Flour.

❸ In large skillet, heat Clarified Butter to a fast bubble over medium-high heat. Add shallots and fillets; sauté 1 minute. Turn fillets; add wine. Cover skillet. Bake 15 minutes or until fillets flake easily with a fork.

❹ Remove fillets from skillet; place on warm dinner plates. Add salt and pepper to Clarified Butter mixture in skillet; simmer 15 seconds. Pour 2 tablespoons of the Clarified Butter mixture over each fillet. Garnish each with 3 lemon slices and a fresh flower for color.

4 servings.

Preparation time: 15 minutes. Ready to serve: 30 minutes.

Per serving: 300 calories, 6 g total fat (3 g saturated fat), 130 mg cholesterol, 915 mg sodium, 1 g fiber.

CRISP FRIED CALAMARI

I started eating squid in 1964 in the submarine service and I haven't stopped. This recipe was a favorite among shipmates.

1 to 2 lb. deboned fresh medium squid, quartered (4 to 6 inches long)	½ cup all-purpose flour
4 to 6 cups vegetable oil	½ cup cream of wheat
2 eggs	½ cup (2 oz.) freshly grated Parmesan cheese
⅓ cup milk	1 ½ cups *Seasoned Flour* (page 170)
¼ teaspoon almond extract	1 lemon, quartered

❶ In large skillet, heat oil over medium-high heat until hot.

❷ In medium bowl, beat eggs, milk and almond extract at medium speed until smooth. In another medium bowl, combine flour, cream of wheat and cheese; mix well. Place flour mixture in shallow pan.

❸ Place Seasoned Flour in resealable plastic bag. Add squid; seal bag. Shake to coat squid pieces well. Remove squid from bag, shaking off excess flour. Dip squid in egg mixture, then dredge in flour mixture.

❹ Arrange squid in skillet, making sure not to overcrowd; fry until golden brown. Place squid on paper towel-lined platter. Serve with lemon wedges and your favorite sauce.

4 servings.

Preparation time: 15 minutes. Ready to serve: 20 to 30 minutes.

Per serving: 500 calories, 26 g total fat (6 g saturated fat), 375 mg cholesterol, 1075 mg sodium, 1 g fiber.

CHEF'S NOTES:

- To clean squid, firmly grasp head; pull head with tentacles and entrails out of body (pouch); discard any entrails that remain in body. Keep head and tentacles together. Pull out and discard cartilage pen (quill) that serves as backbone. With fingers, peel off outside skin, leaving body whole. Rinse body and pat dry. With sharp knife, cut head away from tentacles, keeping tentacles together; discard head. Rinse tentacles and pat dry. Cut body into quarters.

- If you wish, cut squid body into 1-inch-thick rings. Personally, I like the larger pieces better.

- For extra flavor, shake your favorite dry seasoning on the cooked squid pieces as soon as they are removed from the hot oil.

- I also like to fry 6 jalapeño chiles, halved and seeded, and prepared the same as squid.

ASIAN FISH STEAKS WITH FRIED RICE

A snappy-flavored dish that is low in fat and high in flavor.

1/2 cup fresh orange juice
1 tablespoon low-sodium soy sauce
2 teaspoons cornstarch
1 teaspoon packed brown sugar
1 teaspoon fresh ginger
   Dash cinnamon
2 garlic cloves
4 (8- to 10-oz.) fish steaks
2 tablespoons peanut oil
4 cups *Fried Rice* (page 169)

❶ In blender, blend orange juice, soy sauce, cornstarch, brown sugar, ginger, cinnamon and garlic. In large resealable plastic bag, combine orange juice mixture and steaks; seal bag. Refrigerate 30 minutes.

❷ In large skillet, heat oil over medium-high heat until hot. Remove steaks from marinade; discard marinade. Add steaks to skillet; fry until light brown on both sides and flaky.

❸ Spoon and spread Fried Rice onto clean plate. Place steaks over Fried Rice.

4 servings.

Preparation time: 10 minutes. Ready to serve: 55 minutes.

Per serving: 475 calories, 16 g total fat (3 g saturated fat), 225 mg cholesterol, 695 mg sodium, 3 g fiber.

CHEF'S NOTE:

• By placing the steaks in the soy sauce mixture, you are adding flavor to the fish. Soy sauce is very salty, so do not over soak.

SHELLFISH PURSES

These filled pasta dumplings are called purses because they are filled with valuable contents.

¼ cup *Clarified Butter* (page 167)	1½ cups diced crayfish, shrimp or lobster (½ inch thick)
¼ cup finely diced shallots	1 recipe *Pasta Dough* (page 163)
1 teaspoon minced garlic	1 tablespoon cornstarch
2 tablespoons finely chopped fresh basil	6 cups *Chicken Stock* (page 164)
¼ teaspoon low-sodium soy sauce	½ cup thinly sliced scallions
¼ teaspoon ground ginger	
1½ cups *Long-Grain White Rice* (page 168)	

1 In large skillet, heat 2 tablespoons of the Clarified Butter to a fast bubble over medium-high heat. Add shallots and garlic; sauté until shallots are transparent and tender. Stir in basil, soy sauce and ginger; mix well. Add Long-Grain White Rice, crayfish and Pasta Dough; mix well to make large ball. Place in large bowl; refrigerate until ready to use.

2 Sprinkle pastry cloth with cornstarch. Place dough ball on pastry cloth; cut ball in half. Roll out each half of dough until about ¹⁄₁₆ inch thick. Using ruler, cut dough into 3-inch squares. Place 1 level tablespoon crayfish mixture in center of each square of dough. To close, bring 4 corners to center of filling; gently pinch edges to seal. Place dumplings in cornstarch-dusted shallow baking pan; cover with clean kitchen towel.

3 In large pot, heat Chicken Stock to a boil over medium heat. In another large skillet, heat remaining 2 tablespoons Clarified Butter to a fast bubble over medium-high heat. Reduce heat to low. Add dumplings to skillet; sauté 2 minutes. Do not turn. Add enough hot Chicken Stock to cover dumplings. Reduce heat to very low; cover and cook 5 to 7 minutes until thoroughly cooked in center. Stock should be mostly absorbed. Place cooked dumplings on warm platter. Brush with butter; top with scallions.

20 purses.

Preparation time: 30 minutes. Ready to serve: 1 hour.

Per serving: 85 calories, 2.5 g total fat (1 g saturated fat), 50 mg cholesterol, 120 mg sodium, 0 g fiber.

> **CHEF'S NOTE:**
> • Most any cooked shellfish works well in this recipe.

FISH FLORENCE

This recipe is named for my grandmother Florence. She often made rice potatoes for me when I was a child. Her potato ricer is a treasured possession in my kitchen.

4 large russet potatoes, halved	1 teaspoon paprika
1/4 teaspoon salt	1/4 teaspoon salt
1/4 cup *Clarified Butter* (page 167)	1/4 teaspoon dry mustard
1/2 cup diced shallots (1/4 inch thick)	Dash ground white pepper
1 1/2 lb. boneless skinless fish fillet, cut into 1-inch pieces	1 1/2 cups fresh mushrooms, quartered
	1 cup heavy cream
1/4 cup *Seasoned Flour* (page 170)	1/4 cup sherry wine

❶ In large pot, boil potatoes and salt in enough water to cover over medium-high heat until potatoes are fork-tender. Drain potatoes. Shake potatoes in pot over low heat 3 to 5 minutes to steam. Let potatoes steam off 2 minutes. Cover with clean kitchen towel. Set aside and keep warm.

❷ In large skillet, heat Clarified Butter to a fast bubble over medium-high heat. Add shallots; sauté until transparent and tender. Gently stir in fish; sauté until fish is opaque. Turn fish.

❸ Meanwhile, in 9-inch pie plate, combine Seasoned Flour, paprika, salt, dry mustard and pepper; mix well. Sprinkle over fish in skillet; toss very gently to combine. Add mushrooms, cream and sherry to skillet. Bring mixture to a boil; simmer over low heat 4 to 5 minutes or until fish flakes easily with a fork.

❹ With potato ricer, rice potatoes into center of warm plates. Top each with fish and sauce.

4 servings.

Preparation time: 10 minutes. Ready to serve: 45 minutes.

Per serving: 565 calories, 30 g total fat (20 g saturated fat), 170 mg cholesterol, 870 mg sodium, 4 g fiber.

CHEF'S NOTE:

• To rice potatoes, place cooked potatoes in ricer bin and squeeze the hand grips. The potatoes will come out looking like rice. Potato ricers can be difficult to find. Check with specialty kitchen stores to find one for your kitchen.

PANFRIED FISH WITH GOLDEN RAISINS AND THREE COLORS OF PEPPER COULIS

I make this dish when I am showing off my artistic side, by painting the plates with pepper coulis.

½ cup *Seasoned Flour* (page 170)
1 tablespoon chili powder
¼ cup olive oil
4 (8 to 10 oz.) boneless skinless fish fillets

½ cup golden raisins
1 recipe *Three Colors of Pepper Coulis* (see recipe)

❶ Combine Seasoned Flour and chili powder in 9-inch pie plate.

❷ In large skillet, heat oil over medium-high heat until hot. Dredge fillets in Seasoned Flour mixture, shaking off excess. Add fillets to skillet; fry until golden brown on one side. Turn fillets; add raisins. Fry until fish is golden brown on other side. Place fillets on warm platter. Serve fillets with Three Colors of Pepper Coulis. Fry fillets until golden brown. Stir in raisins.

4 servings.

Preparation time: 5 minutes. Ready to serve: 20 minutes.

Per serving: 705 calories, 40.5 g total fat (15 g saturated fat), 185 mg cholesterol, 805 mg sodium, 6 g fiber.

THREE COLORS OF PEPPER COULIS

1½ tablespoons olive oil
1 cup diced red onions (½ inch thick)
3 garlic cloves
½ teaspoon salt
¼ teaspoon ground white pepper
1 cup heavy cream

2 large red bell peppers, baked (page 80)
2 large green bell peppers, baked (page 80)
2 large yellow peppers, baked (page 80)

❶ In large skillet, heat oil over medium-high heat until hot. Add onions and garlic; sauté until onions are transparent and tender.

❷ In blender, puree onion, garlic, salt and pepper. Place puree in large bowl. Stir in cream; mix well. In blender, puree ⅓ of onion mixture with each color bell pepper, one at a time. Place individual colored peppers into separate squeeze bottle containers. To serve, paint plates with each color or put 1 teaspoon of each color on edge of plate.

1 cup of each color.

> **CHEF'S NOTES:**
> • To paint the plates, put each color coulis in a separate squeeze bottle.
> • Serve coulis warm on the side with fish.

BAKED RED PEPPER COULIS

2 tablespoons olive oil
2 garlic cloves, minced
1/2 cup chopped shallots
5 large roasted red bell peppers, stems removed, seeded, diced (see instructions below)
1 tablespoon Worcestershire sauce
1 teaspoon salt
1/4 teaspoon freshly ground pepper
1/3 cup dry red wine
1 tablespoon dill pickle juice
2 tablespoons chopped fresh cilantro
2 teaspoons packed brown sugar

❶ Heat oven to 375°F.

❷ In large ovenproof skillet, heat oil over medium-high heat until hot. Add garlic and shallots; sauté until shallots are transparent and tender. Add bell peppers to skillet; cover. Place skillet in oven; bake 30 minutes. Remove skillet from oven and place on burner.

❸ Add Worcestershire sauce, salt, pepper, wine, pickle juice, cilantro and brown sugar to skillet; bring to a boil over medium heat. Place mixture in blender; puree until smooth. Remove mixture from blender; strain through fine strainer. Store, covered, in refrigerator.

1 pint.

HOW TO BAKE PEPPERS

Place peppers on burner over an open flame or under a broiler and roast until skins blacken. Turn and repeat on all sides. Remove and place in a paper bag. Close tightly and let sit for 15 minutes. Remove peppers and brush off skins. Pull off stems and clean out seeds. If using hot peppers, wear rubber gloves.

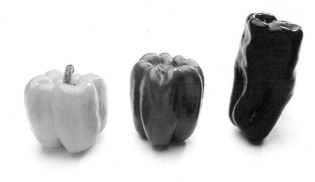

SEARED FISH WITH GARLIC SOUR CREAM POTATOES AND CRISP ONION SHREDS

I first enjoyed this dish in Sydney, Australia, at the Bather's Pavilion Restaurant. This recipe is not as difficult as it looks and is well worth the effort.

4	large red potatoes, halved
2 to 3	ribs celery, cut into 1-inch pieces
4	garlic cloves, halved
1	tablespoon salt
$1/2$	cup sour cream
$1/8$	teaspoon ground white pepper
$1/4$	cup peanut oil
4	(6- to 8-oz.) fish steaks
2	onions, thinly sliced
2	tablespoons cornstarch
1	lemon, quartered

❶ In large pot, boil potatoes, celery, garlic and $1/2$ teaspoon of the salt in enough water to cover until potatoes are fork-tender. Drain water. Shake potatoes in pot over low heat 2 minutes to steam. Add sour cream, pepper and remaining $1/2$ teaspoon salt; mash to desired consistency. Cover; set aside.

❷ In large skillet, heat oil over medium-high heat until hot. Add steaks; sauté until golden brown on one side. Turn; sauté on other side until golden brown and steaks flake easily with a fork. Place steaks on hot plate. Cover with clean kitchen towel.

❸ In same skillet, return oil to hot over medium-high heat. Toss onions with cornstarch, shaking off excess. Sprinkle onions into hot oil; fry until crisp. Place onions on paper towel-lined plate.

❹ Place generous amount of mashed potatoes in center of each dinner plate. Lean 1 steak on one side of potatoes. Top with onions. Serve with wedges of lemon.

4 servings.
Preparation time: 20 minutes. Ready to serve: 1 hour.

Per serving: 530 calories, 22 g total fat (6 g saturated fat), 110 mg cholesterol, 1040 mg sodium, 5.5 g fiber.

CRAB CAKES

With its influence of flavors from the Maryland shore crab houses, this recipe always takes me back to my days as an executive chef in Washington, D.C.

2   tablespoons butter
1   tablespoon extra-virgin olive oil
1   cup each diced red onions, red bell peppers, unpeeled red potatoes (1/4 inch thick)
1/2 cup *Fresh Bread Crumbs* (page 163)
2   tablespoons finely chopped fresh cilantro
1/2 teaspoon salt

1/4 teaspoon freshly ground pepper
1   pinch cayenne pepper
2   whole eggs
1/4 cup heavy cream
2   cups lump crabmeat
1   cup *Seasoned Flour* (page 170)
2   tablespoons *Clarified Butter* (page 167)

❶ In large skillet, heat butter and oil to a fast bubble over medium-high heat. Add onion and bell peppers; sauté until onions are transparent and tender. Stir in potatoes. Reduce heat to medium; cook an additional 5 minutes, gently stirring frequently to keep potatoes from sticking.

❷ In large bowl, combine Fresh Bread Crumbs, cilantro, salt, pepper and cayenne pepper; mix well. Add mixture to skillet; toss to combine. Reduce heat to low; cook 2 minutes, stirring constantly Place mixture in clean, large bowl.

❸ In medium bowl, whisk eggs and cream to a froth; add to mixture in skillet. Evenly place crabmeat pieces over mixture; stir to make mixture consistency of stuffing to bind together when formed into cakes. Cover; refrigerate mixture at least 2 hours.

❹ Heat oven to 375°F. Place Seasoned Flour in 9-inch pie plate. For each crab cake, place about 1/2 cup crab mixture in Seasoned Flour. Turn mixture over; gently flatten to make 1-inch-thick cake. Place on buttered parchment paper.

❺ In large ovenproof skillet, heat Clarified Butter to a fast bubble over medium-high heat. Gently add crab cakes, being careful not to break into pieces. Fry cakes until golden brown on one side. Turn cakes with spatula. Bake 15 minutes or until thoroughly heated and tops are golden brown.

4 servings.

Preparation time: 45 minutes. Ready to serve: 2 hours, 15 minutes.

Per serving: 455 calories, 25 g total fat (12 g saturated fat), 225 mg cholesterol, 1255 mg sodium, 3 g fiber.

FISH, SHRIMP AND SCALLOP FRICASSEE

This is a thick and chunky stew flavored with red wine.

1/4 cup butter
 1   cup chopped celery (1 inch thick)
 1   cup chopped parsnips (1 inch thick)
 1   cup chopped carrots (1 inch thick)
1/2 cup sliced shallots (1/4 inch thick)
 2   garlic cloves, finely minced
 1   cup *Chicken Stock* (page 164)
12   shelled, deveined uncooked jumbo shrimp
 1   cup dry red wine
1/3 cup tomato puree
1/4 cup heavy cream
 2   teaspoon chopped fresh tarragon
1/3 cup *Seasoned Flour* (page 170)
 2   cups sea scallops
 8   fish fillets, cut into 2-inch pieces
 1   teaspoon chopped chives

❶ In large skillet, heat butter to a fast bubble over medium-high heat. Add celery, parsnips, carrots, shallots and garlic; sauté until carrots are just tender. Add Chicken Stock and shrimp; cook 1 minute. Add wine, tomato puree, cream and tarragon; bring to a rolling boil.

❷ Pour Seasoned Flour in 9-inch pie plate. Dredge scallops and fillets in Seasoned Flour; add to skillet. Add chives; simmer 5 minutes until scallops turn opaque and fillets flake easily with a fork.

❸ Spoon 2 fillets into center of each plate; add scallops. Place shrimp around edge of plates. Spoon vegetables over fish.

4 servings.

Preparation time: 30 minutes. Ready to serve: 50 minutes.

Per serving: 800 calories, 24 g total fat (12 g saturated fat), 380 mg cholesterol, 1105 mg sodium, 4 g fiber.

CHEF'S NOTES:
• This recipe is best with sweeter types of fish such as walleye pike, red fish, Dover sole, trout and Arctic char.
• Great side dishes for this recipe include buttered egg noodles and spätzle.

FISH CASINO

Full of color and flavor for a sweet pepper lover.

2 tablespoons butter
1/2 cup *Seasoned Flour* (page 170)
4 (8- to 10-oz.) boneless skinless fish fillets
1 tablespoon olive oil
1/2 cup diced red bell peppers (1/4 inch thick)
1/2 cup diced green bell peppers (1/4 inch thick)
1/2 cup sliced scallions (1/4 inch thick)
1/2 cup cooked diced bacon (1/4 inch thick)
1 tablespoon drained capers
1 teaspoon Worcestershire sauce
1 lemon, quartered

❶ In large skillet, heat butter to a fast bubble over medium-high heat. In 9-inch pie plate, dredge fillets in Seasoned Flour, shaking off excess. Add fillets to skillet; fry until golden brown on one side. Reduce heat to medium. Gently turn fillets; cook an additional 2 to 3 minutes or until fillets flake easily with a fork.

❷ While fillets are cooking, heat oil in medium skillet over medium-high heat until hot. Add bell peppers and scallions; sauté 1 minute. Gently stir in bacon, capers and Worcestershire sauce.

❸ Place fillets on warm serving platter. Top fillets with bell pepper mixture. Serve with lemon wedges.

4 servings.
Preparation time: 15 minutes. Ready to serve: 25 minutes.

Per serving: 390 calories, 17 g total fat (6.5 g saturated fat), 145 mg cholesterol, 745 mg sodium, 1.5 g fiber.

CHEF'S NOTE:
• This is an outstanding recipe for all fish fillets and steaks.

$\mathcal{S}$WEET-AND-SOUR SQUID

This recipe is prepared as close to serving time as possible. I recommend serving this recipe with steamed rice, fried rice or pasta.

8 deboned fresh medium squid, cut into 1/2-inch-thick rings	1/4 teaspoon ground white pepper
1 cup packed brown sugar	2 eggs
1 tablespoon plus 1/2 cup cornstarch	3 drops hot red pepper sauce
1/2 cup rice wine vinegar	1/3 cup peanut oil
1/2 cup fresh pineapple juice	1 cup each sliced carrots, celery (1/4 inch thick)
1/4 cup fresh orange juice	1 cup sliced whole mushrooms (1/4 inch thick)
1/3 cup ketchup	1 red bell pepper, sliced (1/4 inch thick)
1 tablespoon plus 1 teaspoon low-sodium soy sauce	1 bunch sliced scallions (1/4 inch thick)
1/4 cup all-purpose flour	1 garlic clove, thinly sliced
1/2 teaspoon ground ginger	

❶ In medium bowl, combine brown sugar and 1 tablespoon of the cornstarch. In large pot, combine vinegar, pineapple juice, orange juice, ketchup and 1 tablespoon of the soy sauce. Add brown sugar mixture; whisk until smooth. Bring to a simmer over medium heat 5 minutes, stirring frequently to keep from scorching. Place mixture in small bowl.

❷ In medium bowl, combine remaining 1/2 cup cornstarch, flour, ginger and pepper; sift into large resealable plastic bag. In another small bowl, whisk eggs, remaining 1 teaspoon soy sauce and hot red pepper sauce to a froth.

❸ In large skillet, heat peanut oil to a fast bubble over medium-high heat. Place squid in resealable plastic bag with cornstarch mixture; seal bag. Shake to coat. Remove squid from bag; add to egg mixture. Return squid to cornstarch mixture; coat evenly, shaking off excess. Add coated squid to skillet; sauté until squid is crisp and bone white. Remove to paper-towel-lined bowl; keep warm.

❹ Return peanut oil to a bubble over medium heat. Add carrots, celery, garlic, mushrooms, bell pepper and scallions; sauté until celery is transparent and tender. Add 1 tablespoon cornstarch mixture; combine well. Cook 2 minutes. Add ketchup mixture to skillet; stir to combine. Simmer 2 minutes. Add cooked squid and scallions. Simmer until liquid becomes clear and shiny. Remove from heat.

4 servings.

Preparation time: 30 minutes. Ready to serve: 1 hour, 15 minutes.

Per serving: 690 calories, 21.5 g total fat (4 g saturated fat), 395 mg cholesterol, 575 mg sodium, 3.5 g fiber.

CLAMS ON ANGEL HAIR

For this elegant dish, it is important to be organized. It needs to be prepared as close to service time as possible. First make sure you have all ingredients, then make sure you have the proper pans. Have clams cleaned, vegetables peeled and cut.

1	tablespoon olive oil	8	whole cremini mushrooms
2	ribs celery, cut into 1-inch pieces	1	teaspoon dried tarragon
4	shallots	1/4	teaspoon salt
2	garlic cloves	1/4	teaspoon freshly ground pepper
4	cups cold water	1	cup heavy cream
2	cups dry white wine	1	tablespoon freshly grated
3	lb. littleneck clams		Parmesan cheese
1	lb. angel hair pasta		

❶ In large skillet, heat oil over medium-high heat until hot. Add celery, shallots and garlic; sauté until celery is transparent and tender. Add water and wine; bring to a brisk boil.

❷ Gently place clams in saucepan; cover and steam about 5 minutes or just until shells begin to open. With slotted spoon, remove clams and vegetables from broth; place in warm bowl. Cover to keep hot.

❸ Return liquid to a boil; cook to reduce to one-half the volume. Add pasta, mushrooms, tarragon, salt, pepper and cream; toss gently to combine. Return clams and vegetables to saucepan; stir gently. Reduce heat to low; cover and cook 2 minutes. Discard clams that do not open. Serve on warm serving platter. Sprinkle with cheese.

4 servings.

Preparation time: 15 minutes. Ready to serve: 45 minutes.

Per serving: 745 calories, 25 g total fat (13 g saturated fat), 85 mg cholesterol, 710 mg sodium, 6 g fiber.

CHEF'S NOTES:
- If you are a real seafood fan, add cooked shrimp or crabmeat with the mushrooms.
- I sometimes add 1 to 2 oz. marsala or sherry wine with the cream, for a little extra flavor.

ISH STIR-FRY

Quick and easy with lots of flavor. And good for you too!

1½ tablespoons vegetable oil
1 cup sliced onions (¼ inch thick)
1 cup sliced carrots (¼ inch thick)
1 cup sliced celery (¼ inch thick)
1 cup sliced fresh mushrooms (¼ inch thick)
1 cup sliced red bell peppers (¼ inch thick, 3 inches long)
2 cups *Chicken Stock* (page 164)
1 tablespoon cornstarch
1 tablespoon low-sodium soy sauce
1 teaspoon finely minced fresh ginger
3 cups sliced fish fillets, skin on (1-inch long)
4 cups *Long-Grain White Rice* (page 168)

❶ In large skillet, heat oil over medium-high heat until hot. Add onions, carrots, celery, mushrooms and bell peppers; sauté 3 minutes, turning gently to keep from burning.

❷ In medium bowl, combine Chicken Stock, cornstarch, soy sauce and ginger; mix well. Pour mixture into skillet. Reduce heat to medium; simmer 5 minutes. Gently add fillets; cook until fillets flake easily with a fork and sauce is clear.

❸ Spoon Long-Grain White Rice onto warm platter. Arrange fish and vegetables over rice.

4 servings.

Preparation time: 20 minutes. Ready to serve: 35 minutes.

Per serving: 435 calories, 8 g total fat (1.5 g saturated fat), 70 mg cholesterol, 1035 mg sodium, 3.5 g fiber.

CHEF'S NOTES:

• This is my favorite recipe for bluefish.

• Substitute fish freely, but remember that firmer fish fillets work best for this particular dish.

• Leave the skin on the fillets to help keep the fish pieces intact.

• The vegetables look and cook best if sliced Chinese-style or on the diagonal.

WALLEYE AND MOREL MUSHROOMS

The marriage of two delicate flavors in one great dish!

¼ cup *Clarified Butter* (page 167)
1 cup *Seasoned Flour* (page 170)
4 (8- to 10-oz.) boneless skinless walleye fillets
12 small to medium morel mushrooms
1 tablespoon fresh lemon juice
1 cup white wine
2 teaspoons finely minced fresh tarragon

> **CHEF'S NOTE:**
> • Walleye and morel mushrooms are among the great treasures of the Heartland. Both need tender loving care to prepare correctly.

❶ In large skillet, heat butter to a fast bubble over medium-high heat.

❷ Place Seasoned Flour in 9-inch pie plate. Dredge fillets in Seasoned Flour, shaking off excess. Add fillets to skillet; cook until golden brown on each side and they flake easily with a fork. Stir in mushrooms; sprinkle with lemon juice. Turn mushrooms. Stir in wine and tarragon.

4 servings.

Preparation time: 20 minutes. Ready to serve: 45 minutes.

Per serving: 410 calories, 16 g total fat (7 g saturated fat), 160 mg cholesterol, 785 mg sodium, 1 g fiber.

QUICK AND EASY CRUNCHY FISH

The mixture of cornmeal and Parmesan cheese hardens to a crunchy crust when fried.

- 1 cup (4 oz.) freshly grated Parmesan cheese
- 1 cup cornmeal
- 1 teaspoon finely diced fresh dill
- 1 cup vegetable oil
- 1/4 cup *Clarified Butter* (page 167)
- 1 cup *Seasoned Flour* (page 170)
- 4 (6- to 8-oz.) boneless skinless fish fillets, quartered
- 1 cup *Egg Wash* (page 163)
- 1 teaspoon fresh lemon juice
- 1 lemon, quartered

> **CHEF'S NOTES:**
> - Dust fish with your favorite seasoning such as Cajun, lemon-pepper or garlic salt.
> - Serve with sautéed mushrooms and scallops, if desired. Use your favorite sauce or salsa as a dipping sauce.

❶ In 9-inch pie plate, combine cheese, cornmeal and dill; mix well.

❷ In large skillet, heat oil over medium-high heat until hot. Add butter to oil. Place Seasoned Flour in 9-inch pie plate. Dredge fillets in Seasoned Flour, shaking off excess. Dip fillets in Egg Wash; roll in cheese mixture, shaking off excess. Place fillets in skillet; fry about 2 minutes or until browned on one side. Turn fillets; cook until golden brown on other side and fillets flake easily with a fork.

❸ Place fillets on paper towel-lined platter. Sprinkle with lemon juice. Serve with lemon wedges.

4 servings.

Preparation time: 20 minutes.
Ready to serve: 45 minutes.

Per serving: 465 calories, 20 g total fat (6.5 g saturated fat), 160 mg cholesterol, 990 mg sodium, 2 g fiber.

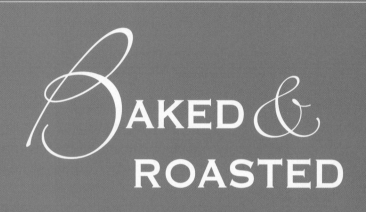

BAKED & ROASTED

Baking and roasting aren't the most traditional fish and seafood cooking methods, but this isn't your traditional fish and seafood cookbook! Put these recipes to work and see how great these methods really are.

Baked Lobster Polonaise, page 118

BAKED GREEN MUSSELS FROM NEW ZEALAND

Greenshell mussels are unique to New Zealand water and are harvested all year round. Make sure to thaw in the refrigerator for 12 to 24 hours.

1 tablespoon extra-virgin olive oil

1 tablespoon butter

1/2 cup each diced red onions, red bell peppers (1/4 inch thick)

2 garlic cloves, finely minced

20 frozen greenshell mussels on the half shell, thawed, liquid and shells reserved

1/2 cup stewed tomatoes, drained, liquid reserved

1/4 cup chopped ripe olives

1/2 teaspoon Worcestershire sauce

1 cup *Fresh Bread Crumbs* (page 163)

1/2 teaspoon dried basil

1/4 teaspoon dried thyme

1/4 teaspoon freshly ground pepper

1 lb. rock salt

1/4 cup (1 oz) shredded Swiss cheese

> **CHEF'S NOTES:**
> • Substitute freely! All types of mussels and oysters are excellent prepared this way.
> • If using fresh greenshell mussels, steam mussels just until they open. Open and discard flat half of mussel shell, keeping meat and rounded bottom for preparation. Strain liquid and use in filling as needed for moisture.
> • For extra flavor and flare, place 1 teaspoon of hollandaise or béarnaise sauce on top of filling before baking. Bake until sauce turns light brown.

❶ In large skillet, heat oil and butter to a fast bubble over medium-high heat. Add garlic, onion and bell peppers; sauté until onions are transparent and tender. Stir in reserved liquid from mussels and tomatoes, olives and Worcestershire sauce. Reduce heat to low; cook 3 minutes.

❷ In medium bowl, combine Fresh Bread Crumbs, basil, thyme and pepper; mix well. Sprinkle over mixture in skillet; stir to combine. Cook over low heat an additional 2 minutes. Remove mixture from skillet; place in shallow baking pan. Cover with plastic wrap; poke holes in film for steam to escape. Refrigerate 10 minutes.

❸ Heat oven to 375°F. Put 1/2-inch-thick layer of rock salt in 3-quart casserole. Set mussel shells, rounded side down, on top of salt; press to stabilize shells. In center of shells, place 1 mussel. Top with generous tablespoon of stuffing; sprinkle with cheese. Bake 15 minutes or until cheese is well melted and stuffing is hot.

4 servings.

Preparation time: 20 minutes. Ready to serve: 45 minutes.

Per serving: 280 calories, 11.5 g total fat (4 g saturated fat), 40 mg cholesterol, 485 mg sodium, 2.5 g fiber.

ROCK LOBSTER TAIL WITH MASHED PEARS AND SWEET POTATOES

This recipe is excellent with large shrimp or scampi. Cut in half and cook in the shell, being careful to remember that they are smaller and need less roasting time.

- 3 sweet potatoes
- 2 green pears, cores and stems removed, cut into 1/2-inch-thick pieces
- 1 teaspoon salt
- 1/2 cup sour cream
- 2 tablespoons packed brown sugar
- 1/4 teaspoon chili powder
- 4 (6- to 8-oz.) rock lobster tails, halved lengthwise
- 1 tablespoon olive oil
  Dash nutmeg
- 1 lemon, quartered
- 1 orange, quartered

❶ In large pot, combine potatoes, pears and salt; add enough water to cover. Cook over medium-high heat until sweet potatoes are fork-tender. Remove from heat. Drain off water. Shake potatoes in pot over low heat 3 minutes. Stir in sour cream, brown sugar and chili powder. Mash potato mixture to form smooth puree. Place in serving dish; cover and set aside to keep warm.

❷ Place each lobster half flat in roasting pan, meat side up. In small bowl, combine oil and nutmeg. Brush oil mixture lightly over meat. Bake lobster 10 minutes. Lobster may need an extra 3 to 5 minutes, depending on size of tails.

❸ Place lobster halves on warm platter. Serve with mashed pears and sweet potatoes. Garnish with lemon and orange wedges.

4 servings.

Preparation time: 1 hour. Ready to serve: 1 hour, 30 minutes.

Per serving: 430 calories, 10.5 g total fat (4 g saturated fat), 135 mg cholesterol, 1220 mg sodium, 6 g fiber.

CHEF'S NOTE:
- Rock lobster tails usually come frozen. Be sure to thaw in refrigerator for 24 hours before preparation.

$\mathcal{B}$AKED STUFFED FISH

A whole fish is a spectacular and ancient dish, naturally full of drama. This is your opportunity to show your creativity and inspire "oohs" and "ahs" from your guests.

  1 (5-lb.) boneless skinless whole fish
1/8 teaspoon salt
1/8 teaspoon freshly ground pepper
  3 cups *Cornbread Stuffing* (page 98) or
      Fish and Seafood Stuffing (page 99)
  2 cups shelled deveined small shrimp
1/4 cup butter, melted

❶ Heat oven to 350°F.

❷ Place fish on sheet of heavy-duty aluminum foil; sprinkle cavity with salt and pepper. In medium bowl, combine stuffing and shrimp; spoon mixture into fish cavity. Brush fish with butter.

❸ Fold sides of foil into tight cylinder over fish. Place seam side down in 2-quart casserole. Bake until internal temperature reaches 160°F.

4 servings.

Preparation time: 1 hour. Ready to serve: 2 hours.

Per serving: 1110 calories, 45 g total fat (20 g saturated fat), 630 mg cholesterol, 1450 mg sodium, 4 g fiber.

CHEF'S NOTES:

• Remove the bones from the ribs through the inside of the fish cavity, leaving the backbone intact to keep fish in one piece.

• A specific baking time cannot be given because each fish will cook differently.

CORNBREAD STUFFING

¹/₂ cup salted butter

1¹/₂ cups diced red onions (¹/₄ inch thick)

1 cup sliced celery (¹/₄ inch thick)

1 cup sliced yellow or red bell peppers (¹/₄ inch thick)

2 garlic cloves, finely minced

¹/₂ cup sliced sweet gherkin pickles (¹/₄ inch thick)

¹/₄ cup sunflower seeds

6 cups diced cornbread (¹/₂ inch pieces)

3 eggs, beaten

1 cup *Chicken Stock* (page 164)

2 teaspoons thyme

1 teaspoon tarragon

1 teaspoon dry poultry seasoning

2 teaspoons Worcestershire sauce

¹/₂ teaspoon salt

¹/₂ teaspoon freshly ground pepper

1 cup diced fresh pears (¹/₂ inch thick)

❶ Heat oven to 350°F.

❷ In large skillet, melt butter over medium-high heat. Add onion, celery, bell peppers and garlic; sauté until onions are transparent and tender. Add pickles and sunflower seeds; mix well. Reduce heat to low; simmer 10 minutes. Place mixture in large bowl. Add cornbread; toss gently to combine.

❸ In another large bowl, combine eggs, Chicken Stock, thyme, tarragon, poultry seasoning, Worcestershire sauce, salt and pepper. Add pears and cornbread mixture; mix well. Place mixture in Dutch oven. Bake about 1 hour.

1¹/₂ quarts.

CHEF'S NOTE:

• Before stuffing a whole fish, cool stuffing in the refrigerator. Then stuff fish and bake. Excess stuffing can be frozen in double-thick resealable plastic bags.

FISH AND SEAFOOD STUFFING

½ cup butter
1 cup sliced celery (¼ inch thick)
2 garlic cloves, finely minced
1 cup sliced green onions
　(¼ inch thick)
1 green Granny Smith apple,
　unpeeled, seeded, cut into
　½-inch pieces
10 cups diced sweet rolls,
　doughnuts, pastries or
　sourdough bread (1-inch pieces)
1 cup eggs (5 large eggs)

1 cup *Chicken Stock* (page 164)
½ cup milk
1 tablespoon chopped fresh cilantro
2 teaspoons poultry seasoning
2 teaspoon chopped fresh thyme or
　1 teaspoon dried
1 teaspoon dried sage
1 teaspoon gated lemon peel
½ teaspoon freshly ground pepper
2 teaspoons Worcestershire sauce
2 teaspoons chicken base

❶ Heat oven to 350°F.

❷ In large skillet, melt butter over medium-high heat. Add celery and garlic; sauté 1 minute. Add onions; sauté until onions are transparent and tender. Add apples; mix well. Remove mixture from skillet; place in large bowl. Add 8 cups of the bread cubes.

❸ In blender, combine eggs, Chicken Stock, milk, cilantro, poultry seasoning, thyme, sage, lemon peel, pepper, Worcestershire sauce and chicken base; blend on low speed 20 seconds.

❹ With large spoon, add blender mixture to bread/vegetable mixture. Add remaining 2 cups bread cubes; mix well. If stuffing seems too loose, add a few additional bread cubes, one at a time, to mixture. If stuffing is too dry, add a little milk.

❺ Refrigerate mixture 20 minutes to absorb liquid. If necessary, adjust stuffing consistency. Turn into 13x9-inch pan; cover with aluminum foil. Bake 1½ hours.

2 quarts.

CHEF'S NOTES:
- If you do not have pastry or doughnuts to use, buy fresh ones. Do not buy pre-made bread cubes; they are dry and tasteless.
- You can also use French or hard-crusted bread.
- If fresh cilantro is not available, leave it out of the recipe.

FISH, POTATO AND CORN MUFFINS

This recipe is too much fun to skip, especially if you have children.

4   cups thinly sliced russet potatoes
12   boneless skinless panfish fillets, cut into 2-inch pieces
6   eggs
1/2   cup heavy cream
1/2   cup *Seasoned Flour* (page 170)
1   teaspoon salt
1/4   teaspoon ground white pepper
1   cup frozen whole kernel corn, thawed
1   cup (4 oz.) farmer cheese, grated
12   soda crackers, crumbled

❶ Heat oven to 375°F. Spray 12 muffin cups with nonstick cooking spray.

❷ Cut 12 (5-inch square) pieces of aluminum foil. Place 1 piece foil in each muffin cup; press to form liner. Spray foil with nonstick cooking spray.

❸ Place 2 to 3 slices potato in bottom of each foil-lined cup; cover sides with double thick layer of potato slices. Spray potatoes with nonstick cooking spray. Press measuring cup on top of potato slices, making a tight fit. Turn and gently remove cup. Place 2 fillet pieces in each cup.

❹ In medium bowl, combine eggs, cream, Seasoned Flour, salt, pepper and corn; mix well. Pour mixture evenly over fillets into each crust. Top each with cheese and cracker crumbs.

❺ Bake 20 to 25 minutes or until fillets are firm and pudding is thick and hot, remove muffins from oven.

12 muffins.

Preparation time: 30 minutes. Ready to serve: 1 hour.

Per serving: 725 calories, 31 g total fat (15 g saturated fat), 460 mg cholesterol, 1700 mg sodium, 4.5 g fiber.

CHEF'S NOTES:

• The key to this recipe is slicing the potatoes thinly enough. To achieve this, use a potato peeler, a sharp fillet knife (because the blade is thin), the slicing side of a box grater, or a mandolin.

• Do not place sliced potatoes in liquid — it removes starch, the binding agent.

• For larger fillets, cut into 1-inch-square pieces that are 1/2 inch thick.

• These muffins are great for breakfast or an easy late supper.

OYSTER CARPETBAGGERS

This is a traditional dish made with stuffed beef tenderloins but I changed the beef to fish for less fat content.

1/2 cup all-purpose flour
1/2 teaspoon salt
1/2 teaspoon fresh thyme
1/4 teaspoon ground white pepper
     Dash cayenne pepper
  3 cups *Fresh Bread Crumbs* (page 163)
  4 (8- to 10-oz.) boneless fish fillets
  8 fresh oysters
  1 cup *Egg Wash* (page 163)
  2 tablespoons *Clarified Butter* (page 167)
  1 tablespoon fresh lemon juice

❶ Heat oven to 350°F.

❷ In medium bowl, combine flour, salt, thyme, pepper and cayenne pepper; mix well. Place mixture in 9-inch pie plate. Place Fresh Bread Crumbs in another 9-inch pie plate.

❸ Make pocket in center of fillets with very sharp knife. Dredge oysters in flour mixture; do not shake off excess flour. Place 2 oysters in center of each fillet pocket.

❹ Gently dredge fillets in remaining flour mixture. Dip each in Egg Wash; coat with Fresh Bread Crumbs.

❺ In large skillet, heat Clarified Butter to a fast bubble over medium-high heat. Add fillets; cook until golden brown. Gently turn fillets with large spatula. Place uncovered skillet in oven; bake 20 minutes or until fish flakes easily with a fork and oysters are thoroughly cooked. Sprinkle lemon juice evenly over top of fillets. Bake an additional 5 minutes.

4 servings.

Preparation time: 15 minutes. Ready to serve: 25 minutes

Per serving: 380 calories, 12 g total fat (5.5 g saturated fat), 205 mg cholesterol, 510 mg sodium, 1.5 g fiber.

CHEF'S NOTES:

- The oysters must be fresh. If they are extra large, only use one oyster per portion.
- The thickness of the fish fillet is important. This fish should be flaky. Cod, scrod, grouper, pike and salmon all work well.
- You may use precooked shrimp, crab or lobster pieces in place of the oysters.

ROASTED CRAB-STUFFED ACORN SQUASH

I am proud of this recipe. It always gets rave reviews!

4	small acorn squash, stems removed, seeded
2	tablespoons olive oil
1½	tablespoons butter
⅓	cup finely minced shallots
⅓	cup shredded carrots
¼	cup dry sherry wine
1	tablespoon all-purpose flour
½	teaspoon salt
½	teaspoon paprika (dark Hungarian)
¼	teaspoon freshly ground pepper
1½	cups heavy cream
1½	cups lump crabmeat
8	(⅛ inch thick) slices farmer cheese
1	teaspoon kosher (coarse) salt

> **CHEF'S NOTES:**
> - For a short cut recipe, simply combine 2 cans mushroom soup with 1 can milk. Whisk smooth. Add crabmeat and fill squash. Top with cheese and bake.
> - Cooked lobster is also excellent with this recipe, instead of crabmeat. You can also use sea legs instead of crab. Either way, you'll still achieve great results.

❶ Heat oven to 350°F. Spray 13x9-inch pan with nonstick cooking spray.

❷ Brush insides and outsides of squash evenly with oil. Place in pan. Bake 25 minutes.

❸ In large skillet, heat butter to a fast bubble over medium-high heat. Add shallots; sauté until transparent and tender. Stir in carrots and sherry. Reduce heat to low simmer 3 minutes, stirring frequently.

❹ In medium bowl, combine flour, salt, paprika and pepper. Sprinkle mixture evenly over shallot mixture in skillet; cook over low heat 2 minutes, stirring frequently to keep from browning.

❺ In large bowl, combine cream and crabmeat. Stir in shallot mixture until well combined. Fill each squash evenly with crab. If squash is not filled completely, top crab mixture with additional heavy cream and stir with teaspoon to combine.

❻ Top each squash with 2 slices farmer cheese. Evenly sprinkle salt over cheese. Bake 30 minutes. Serve with toast points and sliced sweet gherkins.

4 servings.

Preparation time: 15 minutes. Ready to serve: 1 hour, 10 minutes.

Per serving: 790 calories, 53 g total fat (30 g saturated fat), 200 mg cholesterol, 1170 mg sodium, 12 g fiber.

SHRIMP AND SCALLOP TURNOVERS

Vary the size of the turnovers to fit the occasion: smaller turnovers for hors d'oeuvres, larger turnovers for a meal.

1	tablespoon butter
1/4	cup diced shallots (1/4 inch thick)
1/4	cup diced cremini mushrooms (1/4 inch thick)
2	teaspoon fresh lemon juice
1/2	teaspoon salt
1/4	teaspoon ground white pepper
1	cup shelled, deveined, diced uncooked medium shrimp (1/2 inch thick)
1	cup diced sea scallops (1/2 inch thick)
1/2	cup diced sweet gherkins (1/4 inch thick)
1	cup *Fresh Bread Crumbs* (page 163)
1½	cups cream cheese, softened
1/4	cup extra-virgin olive oil
1/2	cup *Egg Wash* (page 163)
1	tablespoon cornstarch
8	sheets frozen phyllo dough, thawed

❶ Heat oven to 375°F. Spray 15x10x1-inch pan with nonstick cooking spray.

❷ In large skillet, heat butter to a fast bubble over medium-high heat. Add shallots and mushrooms; sauté until shallots are transparent and tender. Stir in lemon juice, salt and pepper. Stir in shrimp, scallops and diced gherkins; sauté 2 minutes or until shrimp turn pink and scallops turn opaque. Remove from heat. Add Fresh Bread Crumbs; toss to combine. Place in large bowl. Cool to room temperature.

❸ In another large bowl, beat cream cheese at medium speed until smooth and pliable with wooden spoon; gently stir in shrimp and scallop mixture. Do not break up scallops.

❹ Place large clean pastry cloth on clean, flat surface. Dampen clean kitchen towel with cold water. Make sure to have a pastry brush for applying olive oil and second pastry brush for applying Egg Wash. Lightly dust pastry cloth with cornstarch.

❺ Lay out 2 sheets phyllo on work surface. Brush gently with olive oil. Top

with 2 more phyllo sheets; brush with oil. Place ⅓ cup filling on bottom left hand corner of sheet. Fold bottom right side over to left edge. Fold bottom corner up to right side, forming a triangle. Keep folding triangles up sheet to form triangle package. Place turnover, seam side down, in pan. Repeat until all filling is used.

⑥ Brush turnover tops evenly with Egg Wash. Bake 20 minutes or until golden brown and crisp. Serve hot or cold.

4 servings. (2 turnovers per person).

Preparation time: 1 hour, 30 minutes. Ready to serve: 2 hours.

Per serving: 765 calories, 51 g total fat (24 g saturated fat), 240 mg cholesterol, 1285 mg sodium, 2 g fiber.

CHEF'S NOTES:

- This recipe is also great with cooked lobster or crabmeat substituting the shrimp or scallops.
- Do not worry about the phyllo sheets tearing. Just match pieces and continue on.
- Be gentle when brushing the sheets with olive oil.
- Apply the Egg Wash coating lightly
- If you freeze unbaked turnovers, wrap them in double-thick or doubled-up plastic wrap *and* place in a resealable plastic bag. The dough will dry out easily and this protection is important.

FISH PAELLA FOR THE FAMILY

My first paella was prepared by Chico, a great Puerto Rican cook at the Quinnipiak Club in New Haven, Connecticut, where I was apprenticed while attending the Culinary Institute of America in 1970. Yes, it was that long ago!

1/2 cup olive oil	1/2 teaspoon freshly ground pepper
8 chicken thigh with leg pieces	1 tablespoon Spanish paprika
2 large red onions, quartered	20 saffron threads
4 garlic cloves, halved	4 plum tomatoes, halved
8 smoked pork chops	1 cup whole stuffed medium-size Spanish olives
1/2 cup butter	1 cup whole ripe olives
4 red bell peppers, seeded, quartered	2 cups frozen sweet peas, thawed
2 cups fresh whole artichoke hearts	2 lb. shelled, deveined uncooked medium shrimp
1 1/2 lb. *Long-Grain White Rice* (page 168)	4 cups clam broth
2 teaspoons salt	8 (8- to 10-oz.) boneless fish fillets

❶ In large skillet, heat olive oil over medium-high heat until hot. Add chicken; brown on both sides. Reduce heat to medium; fry chicken 15 minutes, being careful not to burn. Push chicken to one side of skillet. Add onions and garlic; sauté until onions are transparent and tender. Push to one side; stack chicken on top.

❷ Add pork chops to skillet; fry until light brown on both sides. Heat oven to 375°F. Add butter to oil in skillet; bring to a fast bubble over medium heat. Add bell peppers and artichoke hearts; sauté 2 minutes. Add Long-Grain White Rice; mix well with wooden spoon. Simmer 15 minutes. In small bowl, combine salt, pepper, paprika and saffron; mix well to remove lumps from paprika. Sprinkle over rice mixture.

❸ Add tomatoes, skin side down, olives and peas. Place pork chops and chicken pieces alternately around sides with vegetables and liquid. Add shrimp and clam broth. Arrange onions in center; cover with fillets. Return liquid to a boil; simmer 5 minutes.

❹ Place skillet in oven; bake 20 minutes or until pork is no longer pink in center, shrimp turn pink and fillets flake easily with a fork.

12 servings.

Preparation time: 30 minutes. Ready to serve: 1 hour, 30 minutes.

Per serving: 890 calories, 35 g total fat (11.5 g saturated fat), 295 mg cholesterol, 2000 mg sodium, 5 g fiber.

$\mathcal{T}$HE FISH IS IN THE BAG

You can purchase high-temperature roasting bags at supermarkets everywhere.

$1/2$ cup instant potato granules
$1/2$ cup (2 oz.) freshly grated Parmesan cheese
  2   teaspoons chopped fresh thyme
  1   teaspoon salt
$1/8$ teaspoon ground white pepper
  4   (8- to 10-oz.) fish fillets, cut into $1^1/_2$-inch pieces
  1   medium to large oven bag
  2   cups diced potatoes
  1   cup diced red onions ($1/4$ inch thick)
  1   cup diced carrots ($1/4$ inch thick)
  1   cup diced celery ($1/4$ inch thick)
  2   teaspoons fresh lemon juice
$1^1/_2$ tablespoons butter, melted

❶ Heat oven to 375°F.

❷ In shallow bowl, combine potato flakes, cheese, thyme, salt and pepper; toss gently. Dredge fillets in mixture to coat.

❸ In oven bag, place diced potatoes, onions, carrots, celery, lemon juice and butter; seal tightly. Shake gently to combine.

❹ Place fillets in bag; seal tightly. Toss bag again gently; place in Dutch oven. Make slit in top of bag. Bake 30 minutes or until fish flakes easily with a fork.

4 servings.

Preparation time: 20 minutes. Ready to serve: 1 hour.

Per serving: 430 calories, 11 g total fat (6 g saturated fat), 140 mg cholesterol, 1075 mg sodium, 4 g fiber.

CHEF'S NOTES:
• The vegetables need to be diced small to be tender when the fish are done.
• The liquid from the vegetables and fish makes the sauce.
• I like to use a roasting bag in a Dutch oven for camp cooking.

COCONUT-PECAN TROUT

Trout is wonderful here, but this recipe works well with all fish steaks and fillets.

1/2   cup *Seasoned Flour* (page 170)
 1   cup *Egg Wash* (page 163)
 1   cup crushed granola
1/2   cup chopped pecans
1/4   cup coconut flakes
 4   (8- to 10-oz.) boneless trout
1/4   cup butter, melted
 1   lemon, quartered

❶ Heat oven to 375°F. Spray 2-quart casserole with nonstick cooking spray.

❷ Place Seasoned Flour in shallow pan. Place Egg Wash in another shallow pan.

❸ In small bowl, combine granola, pecans and coconut flakes; mix well.

❹ Dredge fish in Seasoned Flour, shaking off excess. Dredge fish in Egg Wash, shaking off excess. Coat trout evenly with granola mixture.

❺ Place fish in casserole; evenly pour butter over each trout.

❻ Bake 15 minutes or until fish flakes easily with a fork. Splash with lemon juice before serving.

4 servings.

Preparation time: 15 minutes. Ready to serve: 30 minutes.

Per serving: 775 calories, 50 g total fat (20 g saturated fat), 225 mg cholesterol, 530 mg sodium, 4.5 g fiber.

PIKE ST. JACQUES IN PORTOBELLO MUSHROOMS

Any white boneless fish works well. You may also make this recipe with scallops or a scallop and fish combination.

1/4 cup plus 2 tablespoons *Clarified Butter* (page 167)
1/2 cup chopped shallots (1/4 inch thick)
  1 garlic clove, finely minced
  1 cup sliced fresh cremini mushrooms (1/4 inch thick)
  2 tablespoons plus 1 cup *Seasoned Flour*
    (page 170)
1/2 teaspoon salt
1/8 teaspoon ground white pepper
1/4 teaspoon dry mustard
  1 cup dry white wine
1/2 teaspoon fresh lemon juice
1/2 teaspoon Worcestershire sauce
  4 egg yolks
  1 cup heavy cream
  4 large portobello mushrooms, stems and gills
    removed
  1 cup sherry wine
 12 boneless skinless walleye pike pieces, cut into 2-inch squares
  4 cups prepared *Great Mashed Potatoes* (page 112)
1/2 cup (2 oz.) freshly grated Parmesan cheese

> **CHEF'S NOTE:**
> • If you do not have a pastry bag and star tube, place potato mixture in a medium-sized resealable plastic bag. Cut a small piece off one bottom corner and squeeze a potato border around rim of each mushroom cap. Dip a salad fork in melted butter and mark the top of the potato border.

❶ Heat oven to 400°F. In large skillet, heat 2 tablespoons of the Clarified Butter to a fast bubble over medium-high heat. Add shallots; sauté until transparent and tender. Gently stir in garlic and mushrooms; simmer 2 minutes.

❷ In small bowl, combine flour, salt, pepper and dry mustard; mix well. Sprinkle evenly over mushroom mixture in skillet Very gently swirl and stir flour into mixture. When lumps are gone, add wine, lemon juice and Worcestershire sauce. Reduce heat to low; simmer 3 to 4 minutes.

❸ In another small bowl, combine egg yolks and cream. Gradually stir 1/2 cup hot wine mixture into egg mixture; slowly add to mixture in skillet. Cook and stir with wooden spoon to make smooth rich sauce. Remove from heat; cover.   *Continued on page 112*

Continued from page 111

4 In another large skillet, heat 2 tablespoons Clarified Butter over medium-high heat until bubbly. Add mushrooms, top side down; sauté 1 minute. Turn mushrooms. Add sherry; simmer 3 minutes. Remove mushrooms from skillet; keep warm.

5 Place Seasoned Flour in 9-inch pie plate. Dredge fillets in Seasoned Flour, shaking off excess. Heat remaining 2 tablespoons Clarified Butter in another large skillet over medium heat until bubbly. Add fillets; sauté 1 minute or until fish flakes easily with a fork. Turn and repeat. Remove from heat.

6 To assemble 4 servings, place portobello mushroom caps, top side down, on baking sheet. Using pastry bag with large star tube, pipe out thick border of mashed potatoes around rim of each mushroom. Place 3 pieces of fish in center of mushroom. Top with 1/4 of the sauce. Sprinkle Parmesan cheese evenly over top. Bake until cheese is melted and potatoes are lightly browned.

4 servings.

Preparation time: 1 hour. Ready to serve: 1 hour, 15 minutes.

Per serving: 1000 calories, 65 g total fat (40 g saturated fat), 435 mg cholesterol, 1630 mg sodium, 5 g fiber.

GREAT MASHED POTATOES

4 to 6	russet potatoes, peeled or unpeeled, quartered
4	teaspoons salt
1/2	cup butter
1/4	cup heavy cream
1/4	teaspoon fresh ground white pepper

1 In large pot combine potatoes, 3 teaspoons of the salt and enough water to cover. Bring to a slow rolling boil over medium-high heat; boil until potatoes are fork-tender.

2 Drain off all water from potatoes. Shake potatoes in pot over low heat 3 to 5 minutes to steam. Add butter, cream, pepper and remaining 1 teaspoon salt; mash until creamy.

4 servings.

CHEF'S NOTES:

• It is important to drain off all water and let steam rise off the potatoes for 3 to 5 minutes.

• It is better to undercook rather than overcook potatoes.

$\mathcal{T}$HE FISHERMAN'S WIFE POT PIE

You may add different kinds of fish pieces, shrimp or scallops to this dish.

- 1/4 cup butter
- 1/2 cup diced red onions (1/4 inch thick)
- 1 cup sliced carrots (1/4-inch-thick half moons)
- 1 cup diced potatoes (1/2 inch thick)
- 1/2 cup sherry wine
- 1/2 cup diced mushrooms (1/2 inch thick)
- 1 cup seeded diced tomatoes (1/2 inch thick)
- 1 cup sliced fresh green beans (1 inch long)
- 2 cup diced boneless, skinless fish fillets
  (1 inch thick)
- 3 egg yolks
- 4 cups heavy cream
- 1/4 cup all-purpose flour
- 1/4 teaspoon nutmeg
- 1/2 teaspoon salt
- 1/4 teaspoon ground white pepper
- 1 teaspoon fresh thyme or 1/2 teaspoon dried
- 2 teaspoon fresh tarragon or 1 teaspoon dried
- 1 recipe *Pie Crust* (page 167)

> **CHEF'S NOTE:**
> • Use heavy cream or the sauce will curdle.

❶ Heat oven to 350°F.

❷ In large skillet, heat butter to a fast bubble over medium-high heat. Add onions and carrots; sauté 3 minutes, stirring gently to keep from sticking. Stir in potatoes and sherry. Reduce heat to low; simmer 10 minutes. Remove from heat.

❸ Stir in tomatoes, green beans and mushrooms. Place mixture in Dutch oven or 3-quart casserole. Top with fish pieces.

❹ In medium bowl, combine egg yolks, cream, flour, tarragon, thyme, salt, pepper and nutmeg; mix well until smooth. Pour over fish. Top with Pie Crust; press to seal crust edges to edges of Dutch oven. Cut small hole in center for steam to escape. Brush crust evenly with cream to enhance browning. Bake 1 hour.

4 servings.

Preparation time: 45 minutes. Ready to serve: 1 hour, 45 minutes.

Per serving: 40 calories, 105 g total fat (60 g saturated fat), 500 mg cholesterol, 700 mg sodium, 4 g fiber.

ITALIAN FISH BAKE

Fish and sauce leftovers are great on hard rolls for sandwiches.

- 2 (2-lb.) large boneless skinless fish fillets
- 1/2 cup *Seasoned Flour* (page 170)
- 1/4 cup olive oil
- 1 cup diced red onions (1/2 inch thick)
- 1 cup diced red bell peppers (1/2 inch thick)
- 2 garlic cloves, minced
- 1 cup sliced fresh mushrooms (1/4 inch thick)
- 1/2 cup dry red wine
- 1/2 cup sliced ripe olives
- 1 tablespoon finely chopped fresh basil
- 1 (28-oz.) can spaghetti sauce of choice
- 1/2 cup (2 oz.) freshly grated Parmesan cheese

❶ Heat oven to 375°F.

❷ Line 13x9-inch pan with aluminum foil; brush foil with small amount of the oil. Place 1 fillet, skin side down, in foil-lined pan. Cut slit in center of remaining fillet, leaving 2 inches on each end. Dust second fillet with Seasoned Flour; place on top of first fillet. Spread open pocket for sauce.

❸ In large skillet, heat 1/4 cup olive oil over medium-high heat until hot. Add onions, bell peppers and garlic; sauté until onions are transparent and tender. Stir in mushrooms and red wine. Bring to a boil. Stir in olives, basil and spaghetti sauce. Reduce heat to low; simmer 5 minutes.

❹ Pour sauce over fillets. Sprinkle with cheese. Bake 25 to 30 minutes or until fillets are flaky at thickest part.

4 servings.

Preparation time: 20 minutes. Ready to serve: 45 minutes.

Per serving: 605 calories, 30 g total fat (6 g saturated fat), 130 mg cholesterol, 2210 mg sodium, 5 g fiber

---

CHEF'S NOTES:
- Most home chefs tend to overcook fish so be careful.
- Sometimes I make a pizza crust topped with slices of provolone cheese for the base. Bake a pizza crust golden brown. Cool and top with a layer of sliced provolone or mozzarella cheese. Place fish and sauce on top and bake as per recipe.

WE ALL LOVE OYSTERS ROCKEFELLER

There are as many ways of making Oysters Rockefeller as there are oysters in the sea. This one is my favorite recipe.

- 3   lb. rock salt
- 6   thick slices bacon, diced (1/4 inch thick)
- 1/3 cup butter
- 1/4 cup diced shallots (1/4 inch thick)
- 1/4 cup sliced scallions (1/4 inch thick)
- 2   cups tightly packed fresh spinach, stems removed
- 1   tablespoon finely chopped fresh parsley
- 1/4 cup heavy cream
- 24 large oysters on the half shell, liquid reserved
- 4   anchovy fillets, mashed into puree
- 1/4 teaspoon freshly ground pepper
- 1/4 teaspoon salt
- 1/2 cup *Fresh Bread Crumbs* (page 163)
- 1   teaspoon fresh lemon juice

> **CHEF'S NOTES:**
> • You can sometimes add 1/4 cup julienne-cut water chestnuts in the last step, for a little crunch.
> • For variety, grate your favorite fresh cheese over the top. You can also add a teaspoon of hollandaise or béarnaise sauce.
> • The filling needs to be thick. If it is too thin, add more bread crumbs. If it is too thick, add more cream.

❶ Heat oven to 425°F. Put 1/2-inch-thick layer rock salt in 15x10x1-inch pan.

❷ In large skillet, cook bacon over medium-high heat until crisp. Remove to paper-towel-lined plate.

❸ In another large skillet, heat butter to a fast bubble over medium-high heat. Add shallots; sauté until transparent and tender. Stir in scallions, spinach and parsley. Reduce heat to medium; cook about 3 minutes or until spinach is tender. Stir in cream, reserved oyster liquid, mashed anchovies, salt and pepper. Reduce heat to low; simmer 3 minutes. Stir in bacon, Fresh Bread Crumbs and lemon juice; mix gently to make a thick filling.

❹ Place oyster shells on rock salt; press to keep level. Add 1 oyster per shell. Top with generous amount of filling. Bake 5 to 7 minutes.

4 servings (6 each).

Preparation time: 30 minutes. Ready to serve: 45 minutes

Per serving: 440 calories, 33 g total fat (17 g saturated fat), 140 mg cholesterol, 1030 mg sodium, 2 g fiber.

FISH AND ROASTED VEGETABLE NAPOLEONS

Seasonal vegetables and fruits enhance this dish immensely!

4 tablespoons olive oil	1 teaspoon dried thyme
1 large eggplant, cut into 8 slices	8 (2- to 3-oz.) boneless fish fillets
4 sweet potatoes, cut into 1/2-inch-thick rounds	1 tablespoon all-purpose flour
4 red onions, sliced (1/2 inch thick)	4 (1-oz.) slices cheddar cheese
4 (3-inch long) zucchini slices (1/4 inch thick)	1 teaspoon lemon-pepper seasoning
4 pineapple rings	4 (1-oz.) slices mozzarella cheese
4 jumbo tomatoes, sliced (1/2 inch thick)	4 Anaheim or large jalapeño chiles, stems removed, seeded
1/4 teaspoon salt	4 large sweet pickles
1/2 teaspoon freshly ground pepper	4 sprigs fresh rosemary
	1 extra-large lemon, quartered

1 In large skillet, heat 1 tablespoon oil over medium-high heat. Add eggplant slices; sauté until golden brown on one side. Remove and place brown side down on baking sheet. Sauté potato slices until golden brown on both sides. Repeat with onion slices, zucchini slices and pineapple rings. Season tomatoes with salt, pepper and thyme.

2 In another large skillet, heat 2 tablespoons oil over medium-high heat. Dredge fillets in flour. Add fillets to skillet; sauté until golden brown on both sides. Remove fillets from skillet to paper towel-lined baking sheet.

3 Cover baking sheet with aluminum foil; brush foil with remaining 1 tablespoon oil. Build Napoleons one at a time. To build each Napoleon, place 1 slice eggplant, browned side up, on baking sheet. Top with 1 slice cheddar cheese and 1 fillet. Sprinkle with lemon-pepper seasoning. Add 1 slice each sweet potato, tomato and mozzarella. Top with second fillet, pineapple and second eggplant slice, browned side down. Stuff sweet pickle inside chile; insert skewer through stuffed pepper. Insert skewer into center of vegetable/fish stack.

4 Bake at 350°F 25 minutes or until fish flakes easily with a fork. Remove leaves from bottom 3/4 of rosemary sprigs; sharpen ends. Remove Napoleons from oven; place on warm plates. Replace skewers from chiles; replace with rosemary sprigs. Garnish with lemon wedges.

4 servings.

Preparation time: 30 minutes. Ready to serve: 1 hour, 15 minutes.

Per serving: 800 calories, 31 g total fat (11.5 g saturated fat), 105 mg cholesterol, 1025 mg sodium, 16 g fiber.

BAKED LOBSTER POLONAISE

The key to this recipe is the Fresh Bread Crumbs. Don't cheat — I'll know!

4 (8- to 10-oz.) lobster tails	1/4 cup chopped fresh basil
2 tablespoons butter	1/4 teaspoon salt
1 tablespoon extra-virgin olive oil	1/2 teaspoon paprika
1 garlic clove, finely minced	1/2 teaspoon finely grated lemon peel
1/4 cup diced shallots (1/4 inch thick)	1/4 teaspoon freshly ground pepper
2 cups *Fresh Bread Crumbs* (page 163)	1/3 cup freshly grated Parmesan cheese
2 hard-cooked eggs, chopped (1/4 inch thick)	1 lemon, quartered
	1 orange, quartered

❶ Heat oven to 400°F.

❷ Split lobster tails with sharp knife, starting 1 inch in from tail end and cut to head end, making sure to only cut through top shell and meat, not through bottom shell. Spread meat open to make a pocket. Place tails in 3-quart casserole.

❸ In large skillet, heat butter and olive oil to a fast bubble over medium-high heat. Add garlic and shallots; sauté until shallots are transparent and tender. Stir in Fresh Bread Crumbs, chopped eggs, basil, salt, paprika, lemon peel and pepper. Reduce heat to medium. Cook and gently stir constantly with wooden spoon until bread crumbs become light brown. Immediately place crumbs in medium bowl; cool. Sprinkle cheese over cooled bread crumbs.

❹ Shape bread crumb mixture into 4 logs the length of the split tails. Press tails flat in casserole; open pockets wider and fill each with 1 stuffing log.

❺ Add water to casserole until 1/2 inch deep. Bake 15 minutes or until filling is hot and brown on top, and lobster shells are orange-red. (Water should be evaporated.) Serve with wedges of lemon and oranges.

4 servings.

Preparation time: 20 minutes. Ready to serve: 35 minutes.

Per serving: 445 calories, 16.5 g total fat (7 g saturated fat), 290 mg cholesterol, 1505 mg sodium, 2 g fiber.

$\mathcal{G}$RILLED

There is a secret to grilling delicious fish and seafood: Don't overdo it! Yes, you have to cook it through. But go too far and you'll dry everything out. You can't "uncook" it a little ... so tread lightly.

Grilled 3-Pepper Fish Steaks with Herbed Cream Sauce, page 136

GRILLED WHOLE SHRIMP IN CAPER ANCHOVY GHEE

The flavors of anchovy and capers make this shrimp recipe truly Mediterranean.

20 shelled, deveined uncooked extra-large
    shrimp
 1 tablespoon fresh lemon juice
 1 quart cold water
 1 recipe *Caper Anchovy Ghee* (see recipe)
 2 lemons, quartered
1/2 cup drained capers

CHEF'S NOTES:
- Headless shrimp and scampi (shells on), larger than 16 to 20 count, are excellent prepared this way.
- This is a great way to prepare whole king crab legs.
- Remove 1 to 2 capers from the ghee to nibble on with your shrimp — this gives a nice salty and tangy flavor.

❶ In large bowl, combine shrimp, lemon juice and cold water; let stand 10 minutes. Drain shrimp.

❷ Heat grill.

❸ Dip shrimp in Caper Anchovy Ghee, shaking off excess. Place shrimp on gas grill over medium heat or on charcoal grill 4 to 6 inches from medium coals. Cook shrimp until shrimp turn pink. Turn shrimp; baste with light coating of Ghee. Cook until pink on other side.

❹ Place shrimp in medium bowl. Cover bowl tightly with aluminum foil; set aside 5 minutes. Serve shrimp with lemon wedges.

4 servings.

Preparation time: 10 minutes. Ready to serve: 1 hour.

Per serving: 250 calories, 22 g total fat (13.5 g saturated fat), 160 mg cholesterol, 590 mg sodium, 1 g fiber.

CAPER ANCHOVY GHEE

 1 lb. whole butter
 1 (4-oz.) can anchovies, oil reserved

❶ In medium skillet, combine butter, anchovies and reserved oil to a boil over medium-high heat. Reduce heat to medium; simmer 30 minutes, stirring frequently to keep milk solids from scorching.

❷ When ghee is ready, butter and milk solids will be golden brown with anchovy flavor. Store, covered, in refrigerator until ready to serve.

4 servings.

PINEAPPLE-LIME-HONEY GRILLED FISH

This recipe mixes flavors and colors for a great taste. I almost like the pineapple wedges the best!

> 4 (6- to 8-oz.) fish steaks
> 1/4 cup diced red onions (1/4 inch thick)
> 1/4 cup honey
> 1/4 cup fresh pineapple juice
> 1 tablespoon fresh lime juice
> 1 tablespoon low-sodium soy sauce
> 1 teaspoon finely minced ginger
> 1 large ripe pineapple

CHEF'S NOTE:

- You can roast green bananas with this recipe. Brush or spray outside of banana skin with vegetable oil or nonstick cooking spray. Place on grill and roast until dark brown to black on all sides. When fish and pineapples are ready, serve with a hot, skinned banana. To eat, cut off one end of banana and squeeze out warm soft banana sauce. Splash with fresh lime juice.

❶ In shallow bowl, combine onions, honey, pineapple juice, lime juice, ginger and soy sauce; mix well. Place steaks in bowl; cover and refrigerate 3 hours.

❷ Cut whole pineapple into quarter wedges, keeping leaves on. With grapefruit knife, loosen pineapple from peel, leaving about 1 inch in center to keep intact with peel. Lay wedges on side; cut yellow center core out (about 1 inch deep).

❸ Heat grill.

❹ Remove steaks from bowl; reserve marinade. Place steaks on gas grill over medium heat or on charcoal grill 4 to 6 inches from medium coals. Generously rub honey mixture over pineapple wedges; place peel side down, on grill. Cook 4 minutes. Turn steaks; brush with additional honey mixture. Cook steaks an additional 4 to 5 minutes or until steaks flake easily with a fork. Brush pineapple again with honey mixture; turn pineapple wedges over.

❺ Place steaks on warm platter. Place hot pineapple wedge in between each steak.

4 servings.

Preparation time: 15 minutes.
Ready to serve: 3 hours.

Per serving: 265 calories, 2.5 g total fat (.5 g saturated fat), 90 mg cholesterol, 215 mg sodium, 2 g fiber.

BARBECUED FISH WITH YAM SHINGLES

This dinner is ready in minutes — full of flavor and finesse.

2	large yams, sliced into 1/2-inch-thick rounds
1 1/2	teaspoons salt
1	quart water
4	(8- to 10-oz.) fish steaks
1/2	cup olive oil
1/4	cup butter, softened
1/4	cup packed brown sugar
1/2	teaspoon nutmeg
1	cup barbecue sauce
1	lemon, quartered

❶ In large pot, combine yams, salt and water; boil 10 minutes over medium-high heat. Drain yams. Refrigerate until needed.

❷ Heat grill.

❸ Brush steaks and yam slices with oil. Place steaks and yams on gas grill over medium heat or on charcoal grill 4 to 6 inches from medium heat. Cook steaks 3 minutes on each side.

❹ Brush tops with softened butter; sprinkle with brown sugar and nutmeg. Top with barbecue sauce. Close lid; cook an additional 3 to 4 minutes. When steaks are medium-well, remove steaks and yams from grill; place on clean platter. Serve with lemon wedges.

4 servings.

Preparation time: 15 minutes. Ready to serve: 45 minutes.

Per serving: 625 calories, 29 g total fat (10 g saturated fat), 150 mg cholesterol, 915 mg sodium, 4 g fiber.

CHEF'S NOTES:

• Sweet potatoes and yams are interchangeable. If you're not a yam-jammer, use sweet potatoes.

• If desired, yams can be prepared after removing from grill. Place yams in large bowl with 1 tablespoon butter and 1 tablespoon cream; mash and serve under steaks.

GRILLED MUSHROOM CRUSTED FISH ON MUSHROOM RISOTTO

Serve this easy recipe at a group gathering — it's guaranteed to be a pleaser.

- 4 (6- to 8-oz.) boneless skinless fish fillets
- 1 cup milk
- 1/2 cup *Mushroom Flour Meal* (see recipe)
- 1/2 cup instant potato granules
- 3 tablespoons vegetable oil
- 4 cups *Mushroom Risotto* (see recipe)

CHEF'S NOTES:

- The Mushroom Flour takes considerable time to make.
- Be sure to use an oiled, wide spatula for turning and removing fish from the grill.
- If the crust starts to brown too fast, move fish to slower side of the grill or turn down heat and shut the lid. It is important to spray the mushroom crust well with vegetable oil to keep it from burning.
- If you do not have vegetable spray, place 1/4 cup vegetable oil on a plate and coat both sides of fish in oil before grilling.

❶ Place fillets in shallow bowl; add milk. In 9-inch pie plate, combine Mushroom Flour and potato granules.

❷ Remove fillets from milk, shaking off excess. Dredge fillets in Mushroom Flour mixture; press to coat well, shaking off excess.

❸ Heat grill.

❹ Spray coated fillets with vegetable oil. Brush grill with oil. Place fillets on gas grill over medium heat or on charcoal grill 4 to 6 inches from medium coals. Cook 4 minutes. Very gently slip oiled, wide spatula under fillets to lift and turn. Spray fillets again with vegetable oil; turn back onto grill. Cook fillets until slightly pink in center or until they flake easily with a fork. Serve with Mushroom Risotto.

4 servings.

Preparation time: 1 hour, 30 minutes. Ready to serve: 2 hours.

Per serving: 760 calories, 35 g total fat (16.5 g saturated fat), 160 mg cholesterol, 780 mg sodium, 2 g fiber.

MUSHROOM FLOUR MEAL

    3 lb. fresh cremini or button mushrooms
    1 teaspoon salt

❶ In large bowl, toss mushrooms with salt.
Place in 3-quart casserole. Bake at 180°F 12 to
14 hours.

❷ When mushrooms are dry, break into small
pieces. Place mushroom pieces in food
processor; grind until flour meal is formed.
Store in tightly covered glass jar.

    1 cup.

MUSHROOM RISOTTO

    ¼ cup butter
    ½ cup diced shallots (¼ inch thick)
    2 cups *Long-Grain White Rice* (page 168)
    3 cups *Chicken Stock* (page 164)
    ¼ cup dry sherry wine
    ¼ cup dry white wine
    1 cup cream
    2 cups sliced cremini mushrooms, stems
         removed (¼ inch thick)
    ½ cup (2 oz.) freshly grated Parmesan
    1 teaspoon salt
    ¼ teaspoon ground white pepper

❶ In Dutch oven, melt butter over medium-high heat. Add shallots; sauté
until transparent and tender. With wooden spoon, stir in Long-Grain
White Rice until well coated.

❷ In medium bowl, combine Chicken Stock, sherry and wine. Add 2 cups
mixture slowly to rice. Reduce heat to medium; cook and slowly stir
until stock is absorbed and rice is almost dry. Add cream to rice; cook
and slowly stir until cream is absorbed.

❸ Add mushrooms and 1½ cups of the stock mixture; cook and stir until
rice is tender but still firm. Rice will appear creamy. Gently fold in
cheese, salt and pepper. Remove from heat.

    4 to 6 servings.

GRILLED FISH KABOBS THAT WORK

This recipe is easier than it looks and is a great way to serve a large gathering in short time.

1 cup *Seasoned Flour* (page 170)
1 lb. boneless skinless fish fillet, cut into 1-inch pieces
4 cups water
1 teaspoon salt
8 small red potatoes
4 shallots
1 tablespoon olive oil
2 large red bell peppers, cut into 8 pieces
2 zucchini, cut into 8 rounds (½ inch thick)

8 mushrooms, stems evenly trimmed to cap bottom
½ cup dry sherry wine
½ lb. thick-sliced bacon, cooked, halved
4 long wooden or metal skewers
2 cups vinegar and oil herbed dressing
2 lemons
8 scallions, root end removed, cut into 2-inch lengths

❶ Place Seasoned Flour in 9-inch pie plate. Roll fish in Seasoned Flour. Place on wire rack; dry 10 minutes.

❷ In large pot, bring water and salt to a boil over medium-high heat. Add potatoes and shallots; boil 10 minutes. Drain potatoes and shallots into colander. In large skillet, heat olive oil over medium-high heat until hot. Add bell peppers, zucchini and mushrooms; sauté 2 minutes. Add sherry. Turn vegetables; simmer an additional 2 minutes. Place vegetables on wire rack; cool. Wrap each piece of fish in one-half slice of bacon.

❸ On each skewer, place 1 mushroom cap, rounded side out. Next, place 1 zucchini slice, 1 piece of fish, 1 bell pepper slice, 1 piece of fish, 1 shallot, 1 potato, 1 slice fish, 1 slice bell pepper, 1 piece fish, 1 zucchini slice and 1 mushroom, rounded side out.

❹ Place kabobs in 15x10x1-inch pan; drizzle with dressing. Cover with plastic wrap. Refrigerate 1 hour or until ready to grill. Heat grill. Place kabobs on gas grill over medium heat or on charcoal grill 4 to 6 inches from medium coals. Cook, turning ¼ turns at a time, until all sides are golden brown and fish flakes easily with a fork. Before serving, place scallion piece on ends of each skewer.

4 servings.

Preparation time: 10 minutes. Ready to serve: 1 hour.

Per serving: 725 calories, 30 g total fat (7 g saturated fat), 85 mg cholesterol, 1905 mg sodium, 9.5 g fiber.

GRILLED FISH AND EGGPLANT ROMA

Be an Italian grill chef with this fun and easy recipe.

4	(2- to 3-oz.) boneless skinless fish steaks
4	slices red onion ($1/2$ inch thick)
4	slices eggplant ($1/2$ inch thick)
4	red bell peppers, sliced into $1/2$-inch-thick rings
8	slices tomato (1 inch thick)
$1/2$	cup olive oil
1	(28-oz.) can spaghetti sauce
$1/8$	teaspoon salt
$1/8$	freshly ground pepper
1	tablespoon chopped fresh cilantro
1	tablespoon chopped fresh basil
3	cup (12-oz.) freshly grated mozzarella cheese

❶ Heat grill.

❷ Brush steaks, onions, eggplant, bell peppers and tomatoes with oil. Place spaghetti sauce in small saucepan on side of grill. Place onions and eggplant on gas grill over medium heat or on charcoal grill 4 to 6 inches from medium coals. Cook 3 minutes on each side.

❸ Add steaks, bell peppers and tomato to grill; cook 2 minutes on each side or until steaks flake easily with a fork. Turn and season with salt and pepper. Cook an additional 2 minutes.

❹ Remove onions, eggplant, steaks, bell peppers and tomato from grill.

❺ Arrange eggplant on clean large platter. Layer with steaks and bell peppers. Spoon $1/2$ tablespoon of the spaghetti sauce over each bell pepper ring. Add 1 steak to each bell pepper ring. Top each with onion and more sauce to taste. Evenly season with salt, pepper, cilantro and basil. Add tomato slices and more sauce to taste. Sprinkle with cheese.

4 servings.

Preparation time: 20 minutes. Ready to serve: 45 minutes.

Per serving: 675 calories, 38 g total fat (12 g saturated fat), 105 mg cholesterol, 1970 mg sodium, 7 g fiber.

CHEF'S NOTE:

• Use your imagination with all your favorite vegetables and spices instead of what I've listed here. You don't have to "follow the rules" all the time!

GRILLED FISH WITH MUSTARD DILL SOUR CREAM SAUCE

Spice up your fish with this traditional French dish.

4 (6- to 8-oz.) fish fillets	1 teaspoon Worcestershire sauce
¼ cup peanut oil	1 cup *Mustard Dill Sour Cream Sauce* (see recipe)
1 tablespoon fresh lemon juice	

❶ Heat grill.

❷ Brush fillets with oil. Place fillets on gas grill over medium heat or on charcoal grill 4 to 6 inches from medium coals. Lightly sprinkle lemon juice over fillets. Grill 5 minutes on each side. Turn with wide spatula. Sprinkle fillets with lemon juice and Worcestershire sauce; cook an additional 3 to 4 minutes or until fillets flake easily with a fork. Serve fillets drizzled with Mustard Dill Sour Cream Sauce.

4 servings.

Preparation time: 5 minutes. Ready to serve: 15 minutes.

Per serving: 295 calories, 16 g total fat (5 g saturated fat), 110 mg cholesterol, 250 mg sodium, 0 g fiber.

MUSTARD DILL SOUR CREAM SAUCE

1 teaspoon olive oil	1 tablespoon Dijon mustard
2 tablespoons diced shallots (¼ inch thick)	2 teaspoons German mustard
1 garlic clove, finely minced	1 teaspoon cornstarch
½ cup sour cream	¼ teaspoon dry mustard
¼ cup *Chicken Stock* (page 164)	⅛ teaspoon freshly ground pepper
	2 teaspoons diced fresh dill

❶ In large skillet, heat oil over medium-high heat until hot. Add shallots and garlic; sauté until shallots are transparent and tender.

❷ In blender, puree mustards, sour cream, Chicken Stock, Dijon mustard, German mustard, cornstarch, dry mustard and pepper. Slowly add puree to skillet. With wooden spoon, stir in dill. Simmer until sauce has shiny clear appearance. Place in clean bowl; cover and store in refrigerator.

4 servings.

CHEF'S NOTE:

• Mustard sauce is also excellent cold.

WHOLE FISH GRILLED IN APPLE BACON

An apple-bacon grilled fish a day keeps the blues away.

1	(4- to 5-lb.) whole fish
1	cup sliced russet potatoes ($1/4$ inch thick)
4	shallots, diced ($1/4$ inch thick)
1	cup shredded unpeeled green apples
2	sprigs fresh tarragon or thyme
$1/2$	teaspoon finely grated lemon peel
1	teaspoon fresh lemon juice
$1/8$	teaspoon freshly ground pepper
1 to $1^1/2$	lb. thick-sliced apple bacon, cooked
1	tablespoon vegetable oil

> **CHEF'S NOTES:**
>
> • For a recipe variation, pour $1/4$ cup barbecue sauce over the shallots, potatoes and fish before wrapping with bacon.
>
> • To cook in oven, bake at 400°F 30 to 35 minutes.

1 In fish cavity, place potato slices, shallots, shredded apple, tarragon, lemon peel and lemon juice. Sprinkle fish evenly with pepper. Wrap bacon around fish, overlapping to form crust; do not wrap head and tail. Wrap tail in aluminum foil to keep from burning.

2 Heat grill.

3 Place fish on fish rack. Brush fish lightly with oil. Set rack on gas grill over medium heat or on charcoal grills 4 to 6 inches from medium coals. Cook about 30 minutes, turning fish every 4 to 5 minutes or until bacon is brown and fish is tender and flakes easily with a fork. When cooked, place fish on clean platter. Remove foil from tail; slice into 2- to 3-inch slabs.

4 servings.

Preparation time: 20 minutes. Ready to serve: 1 hour.

Per serving: 610 calories, 20 g total fat (7 g saturated fat), 240 mg cholesterol, 840 mg sodium, 2.5 g fiber.

GRILLED FISH T-BONE STEAKS WITH ANCHOVY CAPER BUTTER

I love this recipe made with bone-in king salmon or lake trout.

2   tablespoons olive oil
4   (10-oz.) skinless fish steaks
2   teaspoons Worcestershire sauce
1   recipe *Anchovy Caper Butter* (see recipe)
1   lemon, quartered

> **CHEF'S NOTE:**
> • Boneless steaks and fillets work just as well as bone-in steaks.

❶ Heat grill. Brush grill and steaks with olive oil.

❷ Place steaks on gas grill over medium heat or on charcoal grill 4 to 6 inches from medium coals; cook 3 minutes on each side or until steaks flake easily with a fork. When steaks are medium well, splash with Worcestershire sauce. Place steaks on warm serving platter.

❸ Top each steak with 1-inch slice Anchovy Caper Butter. Serve with lemon wedges.

4 servings.

Preparation time: 30 minutes. Ready to serve: 45 minutes.

Per serving: 475 calories, 30 g total fat (15.5 g saturated fat), 200 mg cholesterol, 570 mg sodium, 0 g fiber.

ANCHOVY CAPER BUTTER

1/2   lb. salted butter, softened
1/4   cup chopped shallots
2   tablespoons pureed anchovies
1   teaspoon Worcestershire sauce
1/4   teaspoon ground white pepper
1 1/2   tablespoons drained capers

> **CHEF'S NOTE:**
> • Substitute sardines for anchovies to make sardine butter.

❶ In small saucepan, melt 1 tablespoon of the butter over medium-high heat. Add shallots; sauté until shallots are transparent and tender. Remove shallots from skillet.

❷ Add anchovy puree, Worcestershire sauce, pepper and capers to skillet; mix well. Place mixture in medium bowl. Add remaining butter; mix well.

❸ On 12-inch-long sheet of plastic wrap, shape butter into log. Wrap in plastic wrap; store in refrigerator.

8 servings.

GRILLED 3-PEPPER FISH STEAKS WITH HERBED CREAM SAUCE

This is a hot and peppery way to enjoy fish.

1 cup vinegar and oil herbed dressing	4 (8- to 10-oz.) fish steaks
1½ tablespoons coarsely ground 3-pepper blend	2 cups *Herbed Cream Sauce* (see recipe)

❶ In large resealable plastic bag, combine dressing and 1 tablespoon of the pepper blend; seal bag. Shake well to combine. Add steaks; seal bag. Place bag with fish flat in 3-quart casserole. Refrigerate 1 hour.

❷ Heat grill. Brush grill rack with oil. Place steaks on gas grill over medium heat or on charcoals grill 4 to 6 inches from medium coals. Cook 3 minutes. Turn steaks; cook an additional 3 minutes. Sprinkle steaks with remaining ½ tablespoon pepper blend. Cook an additional 3 to 4 minutes or until steaks flake easily with a fork. Place ½ cup Herbed Cream Sauce in center of each warm plate. Top with grilled steak.

4 servings.

Preparation time: 10 minutes. Ready to serve: 1 hour, 30 minutes.

Per serving: 530 calories, 32 g total fat (14.5 g saturated fat), 185 mg cholesterol, 425 mg sodium, 1.5 g fiber.

HERBED CREAM SAUCE

2 tablespoons herbed vinegar and oil dressing	2 tablespoons chopped fresh tarragon
⅓ cup diced shallots (¼ inch thick)	2 teaspoons chopped fresh thyme
2 garlic cloves, finely minced	½ teaspoon dried oregano
1 cup buttermilk	⅛ teaspoon ground white pepper
¼ cup all-purpose flour	1 cup heavy cream

❶ In medium saucepan, bring dressing to a simmer over medium-high heat. Add shallots and garlic; simmer 10 minutes.

❷ In small bowl, combine buttermilk and flour; mix until smooth, thin paste forms. Add paste to skillet; cook and stir with wooden spoon to make a thick base. Add tarragon, thyme, oregano, pepper and cream; mix well. Reduce heat to low; simmer 8 minutes, stirring frequently to prevent scorching. Sauce should be smooth and tangy.

4 servings.

> **CHEF'S NOTE:**
> • If buttermilk is unavailable, substitute 1 cup whole milk and 1 tablespoon cider vinegar.

OTHER DELIGHTS

Some recipes just defy classification. And that's a good thing! Here are a variety of great fish and seafood recipes that don't fit nicely into the book's other categories. But, guaranteed, these recipes are great!

King Crab and Scampi Mole, page 149

SHRIMP, SCALLOP AND LOBSTER FONDUE

This is a family sport! My family calls before their surprise visits to make sure I have the seafood to make this dish.

4	(8-oz.) bottles clam broth	1/2	cup salted butter
4	cups *Chicken Stock* (page 164)	20	shelled, deveined uncooked jumbo shrimp
5	black peppercorns	20	sea scallops, shelled
1	teaspoon dried thyme	4	(6-oz.) lobster tails, shelled, cut into large pieces
1	large carrot, cut into thirds	12	bamboo skewers
3	shallots		
3	garlic cloves		
2	celery ribs, cut into thirds		

❶ In fondue pot, combine clam broth, Chicken Stock, peppercorns, thyme, carrot, shallots, garlic, celery and butter; bring to a brisk boil over medium-high heat. Reduce heat to medium; simmer 5 minutes. Increase heat to medium-high; return to a boil.

❷ Evenly thread shrimp, scallops and lobster on skewers. Add to boiling liquid; simmer 2 to 3 minutes or until shrimp turn pink and scallops turn opaque. Remove cooked pieces from skewers; place on platters or plates. Sprinkle with lemon juice and your favorite seasonings. Serve with your favorite dipping sauce.

4 servings.

Preparation time: 15 minutes. Ready to serve: 30 minutes.

Per serving: 540 calories, 26.5 g total fat (15 g saturated fat), 300 mg cholesterol, 1600 mg sodium, 2 g fiber.

CHEF'S NOTES:

• We don't know the size of your fondue pot. Add enough Chicken Stock to fill the pot within 1 1/2 inches of the top. As liquid reduces in the pot, add more Chicken Stock to maintain the desired level.

• For a fun addition, place a few clams (or mussels with the beards removed) into the boiling broth and cook until shells open. Remove and repeat. It is important not to add too many clams and mussels at the same time because it cools down the broth and delays the cooking process of your seafood pieces.

• The butter in the broth coats the cooked pieces when they are removed from the stock.

• Poach shrimp, scampi, lobster and crab with their shells removed.

RAINBOW TROUT IN SALT-CRUSTED BALSAMIC POTATO CRUST

This recipe works with all fillets, but they should be no longer than 10 inches or thicker than 1 inch.

- 2 large russet potatoes, thinly sliced
- 1/4 cup fresh orange juice
- 2 tablespoons balsamic vinegar
- 1 cup butter, melted
- 8 (4- to 6-oz.) rainbow trout fillets
- 1/8 teaspoon kosher (coarse) salt

❶ In 13x9-inch pan, combine potato slices, orange juice and vinegar. Let stand at room temperature 10 to 15 minutes.

❷ On flat surface, place 4 (12x10-inch) sheets of plastic wrap; spray with nonstick cooking spray. On each sheet of plastic wrap, place double layer of potato slices, overlapping each other. (The overlapping is important.) Drizzle each with melted butter.

❸ Place each fillet, skin side down, in center of potatoes. Brush fillets with butter. Top each with second matching fillet, skin side up. To cover fillets with potato crust, lift plastic wrap underneath potatoes. Roll as tightly as possible without tearing wrap. Place on baking sheet; refrigerate 1 hour.

❹ Heat broiler. Remove plastic from potato-covered fillets by unrolling or cutting with sharp knife. (Potatoes will be dark brown from balsamic vinegar.) Drizzle outside of each with melted butter; season with salt.

❺ Broil fillets 8 inches from heat until potatoes are golden brown. Gently turn with large spatula; broil until golden brown. Immediately turn off broiler. Leave fillets in broiler an additional 10 minutes or until fillets flake easily with a fork. Remove from oven. Serve with grilled vegetables.

4 servings.

Preparation time: 20 minutes. Ready to serve: 1 hour.

Per serving: 755 calories, 42 g total fat (19.5 g saturated fat), 270 mg cholesterol, 400 mg sodium, 2 g fiber.

CHEF'S NOTE:

- Purchase the largest potatoes available. Slice potatoes with a mandolin or the slicing end of a box grater. A sharp potato peeler also works well. This recipe is well worth the potato-slicing time.

YELLOW CORNMEAL AND PARMESAN CATFISH

This is an excellent breading for deep frying all varieties of fish fillets.

1   cup *Seasoned Flour* (page 170)
1   cup cornmeal (yellow or white)
1   tablespoon dried parsley
2   eggs
3/4 cup milk
2   cups vegetable oil
1/4 cup butter
4   skinless catfish or other fillets, cut into 5-inch pieces
1   tablespoon fresh lemon juice
1   teaspoon seasoning of choice (Cajun, taco or lemon-pepper)

❶ Place Seasoned Flour in 9-inch pie plate. In shallow bowl, combine cornmeal, Parmesan cheese and parsley; mix well. Pour into another 9-inch pie plate. In another shallow bowl, combine eggs and milk; whisk mixture until frothy.

❷ In large skillet, heat oil over medium-high heat until hot. Dredge fish in Seasoned Flour mixture, shaking off excess. Dip fish in egg mixture; roll in cornmeal mixture, shaking off excess.

❸ Place fillets in skillet; cook 2 minutes or until browned, being careful not to overcook. Turn fillets. Add butter; cook until fillets flake easily with a fork. Place fillets on paper towel-lined platter. Lightly sprinkle with lemon juice. Dust with seasoning.

4 servings.

Preparation time: 15 minutes. Ready to serve: 25 minutes.

Per serving: 490 calories, 20.5 g total fat (7 g saturated fat), 170 mg cholesterol, 1080 mg sodium, 2 g fiber.

CHEF'S NOTES:

• The oil needs to be at 375°F. If it is too hot, the fish will burn. If it is not hot enough, the fish will absorb too much oil.

• To add some spiciness, fry chiles after removing stems and seeds.

• To determine doneness, fish should be cooked golden to light brown on both sides.

A MEDLEY OF SEAFOOD AND VEGETABLES GOLDEN FRIED

Make sure the oven is not higher than 225°F so the heat doesn't dry out or overcook the vegetables.

1 jumbo white onion, sliced into 1/4-inch-thick rings
2 large red bell peppers, sliced into 1/4-inch-thick rings
2 (4-inch-long) carrots, sliced (1/4 inch thick)
1 Granny Smith apple, cored, sliced into 1/4-inch-thick rings
3 cups skim milk
1 tablespoon vegetable oil, plus more if needed
2 cups all-purpose flour
1/2 cup cornstarch
1/2 teaspoon salt
1/4 teaspoon ground white pepper
1 1/2 cups *Seasoned Flour* (page 170)
8 shelled, deveined uncooked medium shrimp
4 medium sea scallops
4 squid, cleaned, halved
4 fresh oysters, opened

> **CHEF'S NOTES:**
> • Steeping vegetables in milk gives a vegetable flavor to the batter.
> • Adding cornstarch to the flour in the batter produces a tender batter.
> • Any boneless fish fillets, cut into 3-inch squares and deep fried, make nice additions to this medley. Cook until fillets flake easily with a fork.

❶ In 13x9-inch pan, combine onion, bell peppers, carrots, apple and milk. Cover tightly; set aside at least 1 hour.

❷ Heat oil in electric fry pan or deep fryer to 375°F. Drain milk from vegetables and apple into small bowl. Add flour, cornstarch, salt and pepper to milk; stir until smooth. Place Seasoned Flour in shallow pan. Dredge in Seasoned Flour only enough vegetable and apple pieces to fill skillet; shake off excess. Dip pieces into batter; add to skillet. Fry about 5 minutes or until deep golden brown.

❸ Place fried pieces on paper towel-lined baking pan. Keep hot in 225°F oven. Repeat until all vegetables and apple pieces are fried. If needed, add extra Seasoned Flour for coating. Fry seafood as with vegetables and apple until shrimp turn pink, scallops turn opaque and other seafood is thoroughly cooked.

❹ Place seafood in paper towel-lined baskets. Add vegetables and apple to seafood. If desired, season with salt and pepper. Serve with your favorite dipping sauce and lemon wedges.

4 servings.

Preparation time: 40 minutes. Ready to serve: 1 hour, 15 minutes.

Per serving: 545 calories, 19 g total fat (3 g saturated fat), 110 mg cholesterol, 1190 mg sodium, 5.5 g fiber.

POACHED CRAYFISH PRIMAVERA

I love crayfish! You will too. If need be though, substitute other shellfish meat. This recipe makes excellent broth and vegetables to be enjoyed with your crayfish.

2   tablespoons olive oil

2   cups clam broth

2   cups *Chicken Stock* (page 164)

1   cup white wine

1   sachet bag (see Chef's Notes)

1/2   cup diced carrots (1/4 inch thick)

1/2   cup diced parsnips (1/4 inch thick)

1/2   cup diced celery (1/4 inch thick)

1/2   cup cubed leeks, white portion only
        (1/4 inch thick)

11/2   tablespoons *Seasoned Flour* (page 170)

1   (8-oz.) can tomato sauce

1/2   cup sliced green beans (1/4 inch thick)

1/2   cup sliced cremini mushrooms (1/4 inch
        thick)

1/2   cup cubed red potatoes (1/4 inch thick)

24   crayfish

> **CHEF'S NOTES:**
>
> • For sachet bag, in cheesecloth, combine 1 tablespoon chopped parsley (stems on), 1 teaspoon thyme, 1/2 teaspoon black peppercorns, 4 whole cloves, 3 crushed garlic cloves and 2 bay leaves. Bring corners together; secure with string.
>
> • If you prefer a spicier flavor, add your favorite dried Cajun seasoning.
>
> • You can also prepare this recipe with green shrimp (shells on), clams, crab legs or mussels with beards removed.
>
> • Try making baking powder dumplings and adding to the broth after removing the crayfish.

❶ In large pot, heat oil over medium-high heat until hot. Stir in clam broth, Chicken Stock, wine and sachet bag; simmer 5 minutes. Add carrot, parsnips, celery and leek to pot; sauté until celery is transparent and tender. Sprinkle Seasoned Flour over cooked vegetables; stir gently with wooden spoon. Reduce heat to medium; cook 2 minutes.

❷ Add tomato sauce, green beans, mushrooms and potatoes; simmer 5 minutes. Add crayfish; cover and simmer 20 minutes or until crayfish turn pink.

❸ Place crayfish on platter. Divide vegetables and liquid evenly into soup platters. Serve with hard rolls or bagels for dipping in liquid. Place containers on table for crayfish shells.

7 (1-cup) servings.

Preparation time: 30 minutes.
Ready to serve: 1 hour.

Per serving: 140 calories, 5 g total fat (.5 g saturated fat), 70 mg cholesterol, 490 mg sodium, 2 g fiber.

STEAMED SPINACH, PINE NUTS AND FISH CHEEKS

If fish cheeks are unavailable, cut skin from fish fillets into 1-inch cubes.

1	cup sliced parsnips (1/8-inch-thick rounds)
1/2	cup sliced red onions (1/4 inch thick)
4	cups fresh spinach, stems removed
2	cups fish cheeks
1/2	cup sliced fresh wild mushrooms (1/2 inch thick)
1/2	cup reduced-sodium chicken broth
1/3	cup pine nuts
1/4	cup fresh apple juice
1	teaspoon Worcestershire sauce
1/2	teaspoon salt
1/8	teaspoon freshly ground pepper

1 Heat oven to 375°F.

2 In Dutch oven, layer parsnips, onions, 2/3 of the spinach and fish cheeks, skin side down. Top with mushrooms and pine nuts.

3 In small bowl, combine broth, apple juice, Worcestershire sauce, salt and pepper; mix well. Pour juice mixture into Dutch oven. Top with remaining 1/3 spinach. Cover with aluminum foil; poke 8 pencil-sized holes in top. Bake 30 minutes or until spinach is wilted and fish is thoroughly cooked.

4 servings.

Preparation time: 20 minutes. Ready to serve: 1 hour.

Per serving: 240 calories, 12 g total fat (2 g saturated fat), 50 mg cholesterol, 455 mg sodium, 4.5 g fiber.

CHEF'S NOTE:
• You can substitute salmon fillet pieces for the fish cheeks.

$\mathcal{F}$ISH CORDON BLEU

In French, "Cordon" is ribbon and "Bleu" means first place. This correctly describes the flavors in this recipe.

4 (4- to 6-oz.) boneless skinless fish fillets, sliced (1 inch thick)
1 cup *Seasoned Flour* (page 170)
1/2 teaspoon freshly ground pepper
8 thin slices Swiss cheese
1 cup lump crabmeat
2 cups *Fresh Bread Crumbs* (page 163)
1/2 cup (1 oz.) freshly grated Parmesan cheese
1 cup *Egg Wash* (page 163)
1/3 cup *Clarified Butter* (page 167)
1 cup *Ivory Caper Sauce* (page 170)
1 lemon, quartered

❶ Heat oven to 350°F.

❷ Place Seasoned Flour in 9-inch pie plate. Dredge fillets in Seasoned Flour; place on clean cutting board. Sprinkle pepper over fillets; gently press into surface of fish.

❸ Place 1 slice cheese over 4 fillets. Cover same 4 fillets with 1/4 cup of the crabmeat. Top with remaining 4 slices cheese. In 9-inch pie plate, combine Fresh Bread Crumbs and Parmesan cheese; set aside. Dredge each sandwich in Seasoned Flour, shaking off excess. Press edges of sandwich to seal. Place Egg Wash in shallow bowl; dip sandwiches in Egg Wash. Dredge in bread crumb mixture, coating evenly.

❹ In large skillet, melt Clarified Butter over medium-high heat. Add sandwiches; sauté until golden brown on both sides. Cover; place skillet in oven. Bake 15 minutes or until fillets flake easily with a fork. Serve with Ivory Caper Sauce. Garnish with lemon wedges.

4 servings.

Preparation time: 30 minutes. Ready to serve: 1 hour.

Per serving: 905 calories, 40 g total fat (22 g saturated fat), 300 mg cholesterol, 1690 mg sodium, 3 g fiber.

CHEF'S NOTE:
• To create spiciness, add roasted green chiles to the crabmeat. You could also use imitation crab.

KING CRAB AND SCAMPI MOLE

You can also prepare this recipe, shown on page 138-139, with a rock lobster tail split in half. I serve this dish with spätzle, egg noodles or angel hair pasta.

6	King crab legs, deveined, halved (12 pieces)
6	scampi or 12 large shrimp, deveined, halved lengthwise
1/2	cup diced shallots (1/4 inch thick)
1	large garlic clove, thinly sliced
3	(8-oz.) cans clam broth
1	yellow chile, seeded, sliced (1/8 inch thick)
1/4	teaspoon anise seeds
3/4	cup heavy cream
1	(1-oz.) square bittersweet chocolate, chopped
	Orange medallions

❶ Heat oven to 375°F.

❷ Place crab and scampi pieces in small roasting pan. Sprinkle evenly with shallots and garlic. Stir in clam broth. Bake 15 minutes. Remove crab and scampi pieces; place in deep serving platter. Cover with foil.

❸ Pour clam broth, shallots and garlic into large saucepan. Add yellow chile and anise seeds; bring to a brisk boil over medium-high heat. Boil 2 minutes.

❹ In medium bowl, combine cream and chocolate. Add about 1 cup of hot clam liquid to cream mixture to temper. Add cream mixture to saucepan; stir over medium heat to melt chocolate. Simmer 5 minutes.

❺ Pour chocolate mixture over crab and shrimp. Garnish with orange medallions.

6 servings.

Preparation time: 15 minutes. Ready to serve: 40 minutes.

Per serving: 185 calories, 12 g total fat (7 g saturated fat), 100 mg cholesterol, 415 mg sodium, 1 g fiber.

CHEF'S NOTES:

• The chocolate should not be overwhelming in color or taste. It is better to use too little than too much chocolate. It is also important that chocolate is bittersweet or bitter. Do not substitute semisweet or milk chocolate.

• To make orange medallions, remove the peel and white membrane from a whole orange. Slice orange into medallions and remove any seeds.

FISH IN A RED SEA BAG

I was a cook and baker on a Navy submarine so if it looked like a bag, it must be a sea bag!

4   (4- to 6-oz.) boneless skinless fish fillets
2   teaspoons dried Cajun seasoning
4   (3/4-oz.) slices provolone or Swiss cheese
4   (1/8-inch-thick) slices ham
4   large red bell peppers, tops removed, seeded
2   teaspoons olive oil
1   cup *Chicken Stock* (page 164)
1   cup mustard pretzel crumbs
1   cup diced red onions (1/4 inch thick)
1   green bell pepper, diced (1/4 inch thick)
1   cup diced carrots, (1/4 inch thick)
1/4   teaspoon freshly ground pepper

❶ Heat oven to 350°F. Spray 2-quart casserole with nonstick cooking spray.

❷ Sprinkle fillets with Cajun seasoning. Top each fillet with 1 slice cheese and 1 slice ham; roll up into cylinders. Set aside.

❸ Set tops of red bell peppers aside. Place 1 fillet roll into each bell pepper. Top each with 1/2 teaspoon oil. Using 3/4 cup of the red onions, fill in between rolls and bell peppers. In small bowl, combine Chicken Stock and pretzel crumbs; sprinkle over bell peppers.

❹ Place remaining 1/4 cup onions, green bell pepper, carrots and red bell pepper tops on bottom of casserole. Place filled bell peppers on vegetables; cover. Bake 1 1/2 hours or until fillets are tender and flake easily with a fork. Serve with vegetables.

4 servings.

Preparation time: 30 minutes. Ready to serve: 1 hour, 30 minutes.

Per serving: 345 calories, 11 g total fat (5 g saturated fat), 85 mg cholesterol, 1020 mg sodium, 4.5 g fiber.

CHEF'S NOTE:
• For even thickness, lay fillets flat on a clean cutting board. With a sharp knife, slice into 1/2-inch-thick fillets.

FISH, LEEKS & SAFFRON VELOUTE

I serve this recipe on cold, rainy or snowy days in the winter.

 2   tablespoons butter
 2   cups sliced leeks, white portion only (1/4 inch thick)
2½   tablespoons all-purpose flour
 1   teaspoon salt
1/8 teaspoon ground white pepper
 2   cups *Fish Stock* (page 165)
1/4 cup white wine
 1   tablespoon chopped fresh cilantro
 4   sprigs fresh parsley
10   saffron threads, minced
 1   cup heavy cream
16   (4- to 6-oz.) boneless fish fillets, skin on

❶ In Dutch oven, melt butter over medium-high heat. Add leeks; sauté 6 minutes or until transparent and tender, stirring frequently. Sprinkle leeks with 2 tablespoons of the flour, salt and pepper; gently mix to combine. Pour in Fish Stock, wine, cilantro, parsley and saffron; simmer 5 minutes.

❷ Place 1/2 cup hot broth in medium bowl; add cream to temper broth and prevent curdling. Slowly stir cream-broth mixture into leek mixture; mix until smooth.

❸ Dust fillets with remaining 1/2 tablespoon flour. Add fillets to broth. Cover and simmer 1½ to 2 minutes. Remove from heat. Let stand 5 minutes to steep or until fillets flake easily with a fork. To serve, place leeks and broth in warm soup platters. Top with 4 fillets.

4 (1-cup) servings.

Preparation time: 10 minutes. Ready to serve: 35 minutes.

Per serving: 365 calories, 26 g total fat (15.5 g saturated fat), 145 mg cholesterol, 750 mg sodium, 1.5 g fiber.

CHEF'S NOTE:
• For variation, add 1 cup sliced fresh mushrooms with fillets.

TRADITIONAL BREADED FISH FILLETS

This tried and true recipe can be made with many variations.

1 cup *Seasoned Flour* (page 170)
3 cups *Fresh Bread Crumbs* (page 163)
1 cup *Egg Wash* (page 163)
1½ cups vegetable oil
6 (4- to 6-oz.) boneless skinless fish fillets
2 teaspoons fresh lemon juice
1 recipe *Tartar Sauce* (page 162)

CHEF'S NOTES:

• Add your favorite spices to the Seasoned Flour.

• Use different kinds of bread when making Fresh Bread Crumbs.

• Add your favorite hot sauce to the Egg Wash.

❶ Place Seasoned Flour in 9-inch pie plate. Place Fresh Bread Crumbs in another pie plate. Place Egg Wash in shallow bowl.

❷ Coat fillets with Seasoned Flour; shaking off excess. Dip fillets in Egg Wash, shaking off excess. Coat fillets in Fresh Bread Crumbs.

❸ Fry fillets in hot oil 2 minutes on each side or until golden brown and they flake easily with a fork. Place fillets on paper towel-lined platter. Sprinkle with lemon juice. Serve with Tartar Sauce.

4 servings.

Preparation time: 10 minutes. Ready to serve: 15 minutes.

Per serving: 475 calories, 15 g total fat (3 g saturated fat), 145 mg cholesterol, 1090 mg sodium, 2 g fiber.

POACHED FISH ROLL-UPS WITH ASPARAGUS AND CARROTS

The green and orange vegetables add eye appeal. By blanching the vegetables, the fish and vegetable flavors keep harmony with each other.

8	whole cloves	8	(1/3-inch-thick) carrot strips, 3 inches long
1	lemon	4	(8- to 10-oz.) boneless fish fillets
2	cups cold water	2	large yellow bell peppers, sliced into 1/2-inch-thick strips
1/2	cup white wine	1	cup *Chicken Stock* (page 164)
1/2	teaspoon salt	4	cups *Rice Pilaf* (page 165)
12	large asparagus spears, halved		

❶ Heat oven to 350°F.

❷ Insert cloves randomly around outside of lemon. In large pot, combine lemon, water, wine and salt; bring to a boil over medium-high heat. Add asparagus and carrot strips; return to a boil. Immediately, remove vegetables with skimmer; plunge into ice water to stop cooking process. Reserve vegetable liquid.

❸ When vegetables are well-chilled, roll up 4 asparagus pieces and 3 carrot pieces in each fillet, skin side out. Wrap 2 bell pepper strips around outside of each fish roll-up; secure with toothpick. Place rolls, seam side down, in baking pan. Add Chicken Stock. Cover fillets with enough reserved vegetable liquid to cover fillets. Bake 30 minutes.

❹ Remove fish from pan with slotted spoon. Serve fish, seam side down, on bed of Rice Pilaf.

4 servings.

Preparation time: 20 minutes. Ready to serve: 40 minutes.

Per serving: 265 calories, 3.5 g total fat (1 g saturated fat), 120 mg cholesterol, 280 mg sodium, 3.5 g fiber.

CHEF'S NOTES:

• Use cod, walleye or most any white-fleshed fish for this dish.

• Do not over-blanch asparagus and carrots. Chill them in ice water and remove immediately.

• When poaching fish roll-ups, remember that the vegetables are already cooked. When fish is tender, the vegetables will be hot.

• To create pepper strips, set pepper stem end up. Remove stem and slice across whole pepper, making horseshoe strips 1/2 inch wide. The end pieces may be poached and served.

$\mathcal{F}$ISH KIEV

Exercise caution when first biting into the cooked Fish Kiev — the butter filling is very hot!

1/2 lb. butter, softened
2 tablespoons finely minced shallots
2 teaspoons chopped fresh tarragon
2 teaspoons fresh lemon juice
1/2 teaspoon Worcestershire sauce
1/4 teaspoon grated lemon peel
　 Dash ground white pepper
3 drops hot red pepper sauce
1 1/2 tablespoons plus 2 1/2 cups *Fresh Bread Crumbs* (page 163)
2 lb. diced boneless skinless fish fillets (1 1/2 to 2 inches thick)
1 cup *Seasoned Flour* (page 170)
1 cup *Egg Wash* (page 163)
1 lemon, quartered

CHEF'S NOTES:
- The purpose of freezing the butter mixture is to keep if from liquefying when it is deep-fat fried.
- The process of rolling the fish cubes in flour twice is necessary to form a tight seal.
- It's imperative to use fresh bread crumbs!

❶ In large bowl, combine butter, shallots, tarragon, lemon juice, Worcestershire sauce, lemon peel, pepper, hot red pepper sauce and 1 1/2 tablespoons of the Fresh Bread Crumbs; mix well. Spoon into ice cube trays lined with plastic wrap, filling each cube half-full. Freeze.

❷ With short knife, cut pocket in each fillet, leaving 1/4-inch wall on 3 sides; secure with toothpick.

❸ Heat deep fryer or electric skillet to 375°F.

❹ Remove butter filling from freezer. Stuff one pat of butter filling into each fillet pocket. Roll in Seasoned Flour, shaking off excess. Dip fillets in Egg Wash; let dry. Return fillets to flour; coat well. Return fillets to Egg Wash, then dredge in remaining 2 1/2 cups Fresh Bread Crumbs, pressing gently to coat. Fry fillets 4 minutes or until golden brown and fillets flake easily with a fork. Serve with lemon wedges.

4 servings.

Preparation time: 20 minutes. Ready to serve: 1 hour.

Per serving: 610 calories, 19 g total fat (9 g saturated fat), 205 mg cholesterol, 1335 mg sodium, 3 g fiber.

OBSTER BOIL FEAST

If you are by the ocean, use ocean seawater!

6   medium red potatoes

6   carrots

12   shallots

6   cobs of corn, husks on, silk removed

6   (1¼- to 1½-lb.) lobsters

6   shelled, deveined uncooked jumbo shrimp

3   dozen cherrystone clams

3   dozen mussels, debearded

3   quarts water

4   cups white wine

½   cup sea salt or table salt

3   garlic cloves

2   lb. seaweed

2   chickens, quartered

3   Granny Smith apples, halved

½   cup each chopped fresh thyme, dill

6   large whole dill pickles

2   whole lemons

1   large russet potato

2   cups butter, melted

CHEF'S NOTES:

- If you cannot get extra seaweed, use green cabbage leaves. Do not cut leaves — remove leaves from the core by pulling off individually.

- If you are not a wine fan, leave it out. Add ginger ale or more water. As a farm boy, I also added smoked sausages or ring bologna to the vegetable layer.

- I sometimes add a layer of boneless fish fillets with dill pickle layer. If you cannot get all the different kinds of shellfish, use what is available.

- Leftover meat should be well chilled and removed from the shells. To reuse liquid, strain well and bring to a vigorous boil for 3 minutes.

❶ Place water, wine, salt and garlic in large pot. Add layer of seaweed. Top with chicken pieces, bone side down. Cover with layer of seaweed. Top with 6 red potatoes, carrots, apples and shallots. Cover with layer of seaweed. Top with lobsters, shrimp, clams and mussels. Sprinkle with thyme and dill. Cover with seaweed. Top with dill pickles, lemons and whole potato.

❷ Cover with thick layer of newspaper. Sprinkle newspaper well with cold water, but do not drench. Cover pot with lid or double layer of aluminum foil. Place on open flame or very hot grill. Steam about 45 minutes, giving pot a firm twist or two every 15 minutes. Do not shake.

❸ When top potato is fork-tender and seafood and chicken are thoroughly cooked, dinner is ready. Serve with butter.

6 servings.

Preparation time: 1 hour, 30 minutes.

Ready to serve: 2 hours, 30 minutes.

Per serving: 1200 calories, 50 g total fat (20 g saturated fat), 360 mg cholesterol, 3700 mg sodium, 13 g fiber.

FISH IN A TIN POUCH

This is one of those time-tested recipes that just can't be beat!

4   (8- to 10-oz.) fish steaks
1   teaspoon lemon-pepper seasoning
4   large russet potatoes, unpeeled, sliced
       ($1/2$ inch thick)
4   zucchini, sliced ($1/2$ inch thick)
4   carrots, sliced ($1/2$ inch thick)
2   large onions, sliced (1 inch thick)
2   red bell peppers, halved, seeded
2   teaspoons cayenne pepper
2   teaspoons chopped fresh thyme
4   teaspoons fresh lemon juice
$1/2$ cup butter, quartered

> **CHEF'S NOTES:**
> • This recipe is perfect for a campfire.
> • Use double foil and turn fish pouches often. Keep on medium heat side of fire.
> • When cutting carrots and zucchini, it is important to make the pieces $1/2$ to 1 inch thick and 3 to 4 inches long. This helps in the stacking.

❶ Heat oven to 375°F.

❷ On flat surface, lay out 4 large sheets aluminum foil. In center of each sheet, place 1 steak. Season each steak with lemon-pepper seasoning. Top each evenly with slice of potato, zucchini, carrot, onion and bell pepper. Sprinkle each with cayenne pepper, thyme and lemon juice. Top each with 1 piece of the butter. Fold up foil to make tight pouch.

❸ Place pouches in 15x10x1-inch pan. Bake 1 hour or until carrots are tender and steaks flake easily with a fork.

4 servings.

Preparation time: 20 minutes.
Ready to serve: 1 hour 15 minutes.

Per serving: 690 calories, 26.5 g total fat
(15 g saturated fat), 180 mg cholesterol,
470 mg sodium, 10 g fiber.

SUPPORTING ROLES

Some recipes rely on other
recipes to get things going.
That's what you have here —
the supporting role recipes you'll
need to create as you build other
dishes in this book.

TARTAR SAUCE

1   cup mayonnaise
1   cup sour cream
1   tablespoon sugar
1   teaspoon freshly ground pepper
1   tablespoon fresh lemon juice
2   teaspoons Worcestershire sauce
4   drops hot red pepper sauce
3/4 cup diced strained dill pickles (1/4 inch thick)
3/4 cup diced strained ripe olives (1/4 inch thick)
1/3 cup diced strained onions (1/4 inch thick)

> **CHEF'S NOTES:**
> • Substitute pimiento-stuffed green olives for the ripe olives, if you wish.
> • It is important to drain the pickles and olives well.

❶ In large bowl, combine mayonnaise, sour cream, sugar, pepper, lemon juice, Worcestershire sauce and hot red pepper sauce; mix well. Gently fold in pickles, olives and onions. Place mixture in large jar; cover and refrigerate up to one week.

1 quart.

CHEF JOHN'S FISH RUB

1   tablespoon dried tarragon
1   teaspoon onion powder
1   teaspoon dried thyme
1/2 teaspoon garlic powder
1/2 teaspoon freshly ground pepper
1/2 teaspoon Hungarian paprika
1/4 teaspoon dry mustard
1/4 teaspoon ground allspice

❶ In container, combine tarragon, onion powder, thyme, garlic powder, pepper, paprika, mustard and allspice; mix well. Seal container; store in refrigerator until ready to use.

❷ Rub mixture on fish fillets or fish steaks. Place 2 tablespoons oil in resealable plastic bag; add fish. Seal bag. Refrigerate 2 hours. Grill or sauté fish as desired.

2 tablespoons.

> **CHEF'S NOTES:**
> • The rub will not tenderize fish.
> • Add any spices or herbs you like.

PASTA DOUGH

   2   eggs
   1   egg yolk
   2   tablespoons skim milk
   1/4 teaspoon salt
   1/2 teaspoon white wine vinegar
   1 1/4 cups all-purpose flour

> **CHEF'S NOTE:**
> • If dough is too wet in the first step, add flour 1 tablespoon at a time until you achieve desired consistency. If dough is too dry, sprinkle 1 tablespoon water at a time over the dough until it is pliable.

❶ In blender, combine eggs, egg yolk, milk, salt and vinegar; blend well.

❷ Place flour in medium bowl; make deep impression in center. Add liquid; fold flour over liquid until dough forms. When dough forms loose ball, turn out onto lightly floured pastry cloth.

❸ Sprinkle 1 teaspoon flour on top of dough. Knead dough 15 times, turning half turn after each knead. Place dough in greased bowl; cover with clean kitchen towel. Let rest 1 hour or overnight in refrigerator.

❹ Roll dough out onto lightly floured pastry cloth into desired thickness and shape.

   4 servings.

FRESH BREAD CRUMBS

   1   (1-lb.) loaf white bread, sliced, crust removed, halved

❶ Place bread pieces, 4 at a time, in food processor; crumble at medium speed. Place crumbs in large bowl. Repeat with remaining bread. For different flavors, use white, whole wheat bread, light rye bread or pumpernickel bread.

   8 cups.

EGG WASH

   2   eggs
   1/4 cup milk

❶ Break eggs into large bowl. Whisk in milk until frothy.

   3/4 cup.

> **CHEF'S NOTE:**
> • Never keep Egg Wash after use. It is a medium for bacteria. If you need only a small amount, make half a batch.

COURT BOUILLON (VEGETABLE STOCK)

3½   quarts water
1   quart dry white wine
1   teaspoon salt
2   garlic cloves, halved
8   sprigs fresh parsley
3   whole black peppercorns
2   sprigs fresh thyme or 1 teaspoon dried
2   sprigs fresh tarragon or ½ teaspoon dried
2   bay leaves
1   cup diced carrots (1 inch thick)
1   cup diced red onions (1 inch thick)
1   cup diced celery (1 inch thick)

> **CHEF'S NOTES:**
> • Use stock to poach or boil fish and shellfish.
> • To intensify the flavor, cook down the liquid until it is reduced by half.

❶ In large pot, bring water, wine and salt to a boil over medium-high heat. Stir in peppercorns, thyme, tarragon, bay leaves, carrots, onion and celery. Reduce heat; simmer 1 hour.

❷ Place pot on wire rack; cool to room temperature. Strain stock through fine strainer into glass container. Cover; store in refrigerator until needed.

3 quarts.

CHICKEN STOCK

3½   lb. chicken wings or 1 small stewing hen
2   cups diced onions
1½   cup diced celery
1½   cup diced carrots
4   quarts water
1   sachet bag (page 145, Chef's Notes)

❶ In large pot, combine chicken wings, onions, celery, carrots, water and sachet bag. Simmer over low heat 3½ hours, skimming off fat and foam from time to time. Remove from heat; strain.

❷ Return only liquid to pot; return to a fast boil. Boil until liquid is reduced by half. Skim off fat; strain. Cool. Store in refrigerator.

2 quarts.

> **CHEF'S NOTE:**
> • Remove meat from bones and use for sandwiches and salads.

RICE PILAF

1½   tablespoons butter
2   tablespoons diced red onions (¼ inch thick)
1   cup *Long-Grain White Rice* (page 168)
2   cups *Chicken Stock* (page 164)
¼   teaspoon salt
⅛   teaspoon freshly ground pepper
2   bay leaves

❶ Heat oven to 350°F.

❷ In Dutch oven, melt butter over medium-high heat. Add onions; sauté until onions are transparent and tender. Add Long-Grain White Rice; stir with wooden spoon 30 seconds to coat well. Add Chicken Stock, salt, pepper and bay leaves; bring to a boil. Turn rice into 3-quart casserole. Cover with aluminum foil. Punch 8 to 10 holes in foil.

❸ Bake 45 minutes. When pilaf is done, bay leaves will be on top, liquid evaporated and rice tender. Discard bay leaves.

4 servings.

FISH STOCK (VELOUTE)

2   teaspoons vegetable oil
1   cup sliced carrots (¼ inch thick)
2   cups sliced onions (¼ inch thick)
1   cup sliced fresh fennel (¼ inch thick)
2   cups sliced celery (¼ inch thick)
1   cup sliced mushrooms (¼ inch thick)
5   lb. fish bones, skin on
1   sachet bag (page 145, Chef's Notes)
2   cups dry white wine
5   quarts cold water

❶ In large pot, heat oil over medium-high heat until hot. Add carrots, onions, fennel, celery and mushrooms; cook 7 minutes. Add fish, Sachet Bag, wine and water; reduce heat to low and simmer until liquid is reduced by half. Water should just barely bubble. Skim off foam. Gently stir with wooden spoon making sure nothing is stuck on bottom of pot.

❷ With ladle, remove foam from surface; strain liquid. Strain a second time through doubled cheesecloth or clean kitchen towel.

1 quart.

EASY CAESAR DRESSING

3/4 cup red wine vinegar

4 oz. anchovy fillets in oil

2 garlic cloves, finely minced

1 tablespoon freshly ground pepper

1 tablespoon prepared yellow mustard

2 tablespoons Worcestershire sauce

1 teaspoon chicken base

2 teaspoon fresh lemon juice

4 drops hot red pepper sauce

3 cups olive oil

1/2 cup (2 oz.) freshly grated Parmesan cheese

❶ In blender, combine vinegar, anchovy fillets, garlic, pepper, mustard, Worcestershire sauce, chicken base, lemon juice and hot red pepper sauce; puree.

❷ In small saucepan, heat oil to 140°F. Check temperature with food thermometer.

❸ Place 1 piece aluminum foil on top of blender; make a deep pocket. Punch small hole (1/16-inch diameter) in bottom of pocket. Turn blender on high speed; pour warm oil into foil pocket. The dressing will thicken.

❹ Place dressing in storage container. Add Parmesan cheese; combine well.

Makes 1 quart.

CHEF'S NOTE:
- Heating the oil and pouring it through a small hole creates an emulsion that keeps the salad dressing from separating.

PICKLING SPICE BAG

3 tablespoons pickling spice

1 (8-inch) square cheesecloth

1 butcher string

❶ Place spices in center of cheesecloth. Gather corners of cheesecloth together; fasten string near top, leaving room for liquid to circulate through spices. Cut off extra cheesecloth on top of bag.

1 spice bag.

CHEF'S NOTE:
- The bag lets you remove spices from the liquid.

PIE CRUST

    2   cups all-purpose flour
    1   teaspoon salt
1¼   cups shortening
 ⅔   cup cold water

❶ Heat oven to 350°F.

❷ In large bowl, combine flour and salt. Cut in shortening to make marble-size pieces. Add water; lightly toss to make dough. Combine dough just enough to hold together. Roll out crust on flour-dusted pastry cloth.

❸ For pie shells, prick crust with fork. Gently shake to shrink dough. Place dough in 2 (9-inch) pie pans. Trim excess dough from edges. Place pans in oven upside down. This keeps pies from blistering and bubbling. Bake 15 to 18 minutes.

2 pie crusts.

CHEF'S NOTES:

• To make double-crust pies, the bottom pie crust should weigh 8 oz. The top crust should weigh 7 oz. for a 9-inch pie plate. Always shake crust before putting it in the pie plate to prevent crust from shrinking during baking. Cut leftover dough into 8-oz. pieces and freeze in individual bags. Thaw in refrigerator.

• Measure flour accurately. Adding too much flour will make the crust tough.

CLARIFIED BUTTER

    2   cups butter

❶ In large saucepan, melt butter over low heat. Remove all foam which rises to top of liquid. Remove from heat; let stand until all milk solids have fallen to bottom of saucepan. With ladle, remove all clear Clarified Butter; place in glass container. Refrigerate until needed.

1½ cups.

CHEF'S NOTES:

• I prefer to use half margarine and butter. The margarine will increase the smoke point temperature, allowing the liquid to be heated to a higher temperature without burning.

• This is sometimes known as "drawn butter."

GRITS SUPREME

1/4 cup butter
1/2 cup diced shallots (1/4 inch thick)
 1 cup *Chicken Stock* (page 164)
 2 cups heavy cream
 1 teaspoon poultry seasoning

1/2 teaspoon salt
1/4 teaspoon ground white pepper
 1 cup uncooked grits
1/2 cup (2 oz.) freshly grated
    Parmesan cheese

❶ In large pot, melt butter over medium-high heat. Add shallots; sauté until transparent and tender. Add Chicken Stock, cream, poultry seasoning, salt and pepper; mix well. Slowly add Grits Supreme; stir with a wooden spoon to avoid scorching.

❷ Reduce heat to low; simmer 5 minutes. Add cheese; cook an additional 5 minutes. Cover to keep hot until serving.

4 to 6 servings.

CHEF'S NOTES:

• To make grilled grit cakes, place warm cooked grits in a buttered shallow baking pan. Refrigerate until cold. Cut into squares or cookie cutter shapes. To cook, sauté in butter until golden brown on both sides.

LONG-GRAIN WHITE RICE

 2 cups long-grain white rice
 4 cups water
 1 teaspoon salt

❶ Heat oven to 350°F.

❷ Place rice in large, deep bowl. With cold water running, add water, letting water rise slowly over rice to fill bowl. Stir rice with long-handled spoon. Discard hulls and bad kernels. Drain rice in strainer.

❸ Place rice in 8-inch square cake pan. In medium bowl, combine 4 cups cold water and salt. Pour over rice. Cover pan with aluminum foil; poke 12 small holes into foil for steam to escape.

❹ Bake 1 hour or until water has evaporated and rice is tender and sticky. Remove foil; fluff with fork. For sticky rice, leave foil cover on when removed from oven.

4 servings.

CHEF'S NOTE:

• Cook short- and medium-grain white rice the same way.

FRIED RICE

2	tablespoons peanut oil		4	cups cooked *Long-Grain White Rice* (page 168)
1	cup fresh sweet peas		1	cup fresh bean sprouts
1/2	cup sliced red onions (1/4 inch thick)		1 1/2	tablespoons low-sodium soy sauce
1/2	cup sliced celery (1/2 inch thick)		4	eggs, beaten
1/2	cup sliced red or green bell peppers (1/8 inch strips)		1/2	cup sliced green onions (1/4 inch)

❶ In large skillet, heat oil over medium-high heat until hot. Add peas, red onions, celery and bell pepper; sauté until onions are transparent and tender. Add Long-Grain White Rice; toss. Stir in bean sprouts and one-half of the soy sauce.

❷ In small bowl, combine remaining soy sauce and beaten eggs. With spatula, push rice mixture to one side of skillet; add eggs slowly to other side. Stir in green onions. Cook and stir until eggs are scrambled, but still until soft.

4 to 6 servings.

CHEF'S NOTES:

• If canned bean sprouts are substituted, be sure to drain well before adding.

• Try adding 2 tomatoes cut into 8 wedges to scramble the eggs.

ROUX

1	lb. butter
1	lb. all-purpose flour

❶ Heat oven to 375°F.

❷ Heat butter in 2-quart casserole until melted; stir in flour. Bake 1 hour, stirring mixture every 15 minutes until golden brown and consistency of sand.

3 cups.

MELBA SAUCE

$1/2$ cup currant jelly
1 cup sieved raspberries
$1/2$ cup sugar
1 teaspoon cornstarch
$1/8$ teaspoon salt

1️⃣ In top of double broiler, bring jelly and raspberries to a boil over medium-high heat.

2️⃣ Stir in sugar, cornstarch and salt. Cook until thick and clear, stirring frequently. Remove from heat; refrigerate until serving time.

$1^{3}/4$ cups.

SEASONED FLOUR

1 cup all-purpose flour
2 teaspoons salt
$1/8$ teaspoon ground white pepper

1️⃣ In medium bowl, combine flour, salt and pepper.

1 cup.

CHEF'S NOTES:
- White pepper means that the flour does not appear to have black flecks.
- Never reuse excess flour.

IVORY CAPER SAUCE

$1^{1}/2$ tablespoons butter
$1/4$ cup diced shallots ($1/4$ inch thick)
1 tablespoon all-purpose flour
$1/3$ cup dry white wine
1 teaspoon fresh lemon juice
1 pinch ground white pepper
1 large bay leaf
$1/2$ cup heavy cream
$1/4$ cup drained capers

CHEF'S NOTES:
- Do not reduce the liquid in the first stages of preparing this sauce. Be careful!
- Serve the sauce as soon as possible after preparing.
- For a richer flavor and color, add 2 tablespoons fresh fish roe after the cream has thickened.

1️⃣ In large skillet, melt butter over medium-high heat. Add shallots; sauté until transparent and tender. With wooden spoon, stir in flour. Reduce heat to medium; cook 2 minutes.

2️⃣ Reduce heat to low. Add wine, lemon juice, pepper and bay leaf to; simmer 5 minutes. Do not boil. Remove and discard bay leaf. Stir in cream and capers; simmer until cream thickens.

4 servings.

PHYLLO DOUGH

   1   cup cold water
 1/2 teaspoon salt
   3   tablespoons vegetable oil
   3   cups bread flour
   2   cups cornstarch

❶ In large mixer bowl, combine water and salt. Add oil and flour; mix 10 minutes on low speed until dough is shiny and elastic.

❷ Very lightly oil another large bowl. Shape dough into round loaf; place in bowl. Cover with clean kitchen towel; let rest 1 hour. Sprinkle pastry cloth with 2 teaspoons of the cornstarch. Turn bowl upside down to release dough. Cut dough into 8 equal slices. Place generous amount of cornstarch in small pile.

❸ Place dough, 1 piece at a time, in cornstarch; shape into small flat disk using palm of hand.

❹ Place generous amount of cornstarch in center of pastry cloth. Roll each disk of dough, one at a time, into 10-inch diameter. Layer each piece into stack with generous amount of cornstarch in between. Cover with another clean kitchen towel. Let rest 1 hour.

❺ With palm of your hand, press around edge of disks, using firm even pressure. Turn disks over. From center out, press with flat open hand to make smooth disk. Press, starting from center, each way. Using rolling pin with even light to medium pressure, make X-pattern. Roll dough as thin as possible. After each X motion, gently shake edges to relax dough. If dough starts to stick to cloth or rolling pin, add a little more cornstarch. Stop rolling before dough starts to tear.

❻ To lift dough; place rod gently under dough in center. Gently lift and set rod on top of 2 tall cereal boxes. To slightly dry, place on a cornstarch-dusted baker's cloth. Place all sheets on top of each other with cornstarch in between. Cover and set aside for use. Use as soon as possible.

10 to 12 phyllo sheets.

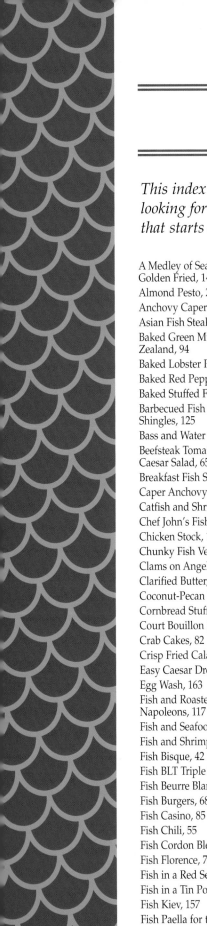

RECIPE INDEX

This index lists every recipe in Fish & Seafood Masterpieces *by name. If you're looking for a specific recipe but can't recall the exact name, turn to the General Index that starts on page 173.*

GENERAL INDEX

There are several ways to use this helpful index. First — you can find recipes by name. If you don't know a recipe's specific name but recall a main ingredient or the cooking technique, look under that heading and all the related recipes will be listed; scan for the recipe you want. If you have a fish, ingredient or cooking technique in mind and want to find a great recipe for it, look under that heading as well to find a list of recipes to choose from. Finally — you can use this general index to find a summary of the recipes in each chapter of the book (starters, soups & chowders, baked & roasted, grilled, etc.).